DENIS COMPTON

Cricketing Genius

Peter West

Stanley Paul
London Sydney Auckland Johannesburg

Stanley Paul and Co. Ltd

An imprint of Century Hutchinson Ltd

Brookmount House, 62–65 Chandos Place
Covent Garden, London WC2N 4NW

Century Hutchinson Australia (Pty) Ltd
20 Alfred Street, Milsons Point, Sydney 2061

Century Hutchinson New Zealand Limited
191 Archers Road, PO Box 40–086, Glenfield, Auckland 10

Century Hutchinson South Africa (Pty) Ltd
PO Box 337, Bergvlei, 2012 South Africa

First published in 1989

Copyright © Peter West 1989

Set in Baskerville 11/13pt by Input Typesetting Ltd, London.

Printed and bound in Great Britain by Mackays Ltd

British Library Cataloguing in Publication Data

West, Peter
  Denis Compton: a biography.
  1. Cricket. Compton, Denis 1918–
  I. Title
  796.35′8′0924

ISBN 0 09 1737885

Contents

Preface

E.W. SWANTON penned a characteristically perceptive vignette about him, *Denis Compton – A Cricket Sketch*, when Compton was at the height of his fame in 1947. In 1971 Ian Peebles wrote a delightful biography, *Denis Compton*, which concentrated in its relatively modest length on his subject's cricketing skills. Denis himself has put his name to several books of his own as well as to one in association with Bill Edrich. But only Denis, I believe, has written about his days on the football as well as the cricket field.

All of those books were written quite some time ago, and no one has sought to bring the story up to date with some account of his activities after his retirement from full-time cricket at the end of the 1957 season.

It makes sense, I think, to write of his lustrous cricket career in chronological order. I have also thought it might be helpful to younger readers if I set his achievements against what was happening at the time in Middlesex and England cricket. I hope that to a passable extent this can provide some story of England's cricketing progress during the Compton years.

Finding a logical place for the other half of a versatile sporting life has been more difficult. His finest days on the football field were spent during the years of the war and, although his career with Arsenal was to continue for several seasons afterwards, culminating with the FA Cup Final in 1950, I have decided, for better or for worse, to put the chapter immediately after a report of his years in the Army.

In my research for this biography I made contact with several of Denis Compton's greatest footballing contemporaries and with many more of those who played cricket with or against him, including some in the southern hemisphere. Their names will figure on the pages ahead and I am very grateful to them all for the unstinting help they have given me. They have confirmed some old stories well worth re-telling, put me right on others and supplied what I hope will be a number of seldom heard anecdotes.

For valuable information I have consulted the following books: *Testing Time for England, Playing for England, In Sun and Shadow, End of an Innings* (all by Denis Compton); *Cricket and All That* (by Denis Compton and Bill Edrich); *Elusive Victory* and *Report from South Africa 1956/57* (by E. W. Swanton); *Australia '55* (by Alan Ross) and *Lord's 1787–1945* (by Sir Pelham Warner).

Wisden, I need hardly say, has been a *sine qua non*, and I have also been much indebted to Bill Frindall's *Wisden Book of Test Cricket* and to Christopher Martin-Jenkins's *The Complete Who's Who of Test Cricketers*. I might immodestly add that my own accounts of the Australian tours of England in 1953 and 1956, in *The Fight for the Ashes* series, came in quite handy. My thanks, too, to Matthew Engel for his penetrating account in *Wisden* of an MCC special general meeting in 1983.

On the football front, Jack Rollin's *Soccer at War* has been an invaluable source of information and I am also grateful for the help of Mr Peter Williams of Newport. Finally, I want to express my thanks to the statistician and author, Derek Lodge, not only for supplying a factual appendix and supervising the index, but also for helping me with some other matters of important detail.

Photographic acknowledgement
The author and publishers would like to thank the following for permission to reproduce their copyright photographs:
Keystone Collection, Popperfoto, Sport & General, Patrick Eagar, *Melbourne Herald-Sun, Hendon Times*, Arsenal FC, Andy Wilson, Nick Royds/HVR.

Nonpareil

THERE HAVE BEEN many great batsmen in the history of cricket but Denis Compton was something very special. He was one of my cricketing heroes when I was still at school in the years leading up to the war, and so he remains, half a century on, after the rare pleasures he vouchsafed on the field and the comradeship of summers spent working together for BBC television cricket. He was a *nonpareil* – a 'one-off' – and I do not think we can hope to see his like again.

Genius, as we all know, is a different thing to mere talent, however shining; it is a gift, an exalted power to stimulate expression, invention, originality. I cannot believe that the cricket world has seen, or will see, a batsman with such ability to improvise, to ad-lib his own script and, in freely dispensing his favours, to share them so enjoyably with his audience.

When Denis went out to bat even hardened old pros in the dressing room would come out on to the balcony to see what might transpire. This would happen just as regularly in the second half of his career when he could be chained by an arthritic, much manipulated and restrictive right knee. I remember an old England player, reminiscing about days and heroes of yore, being asked by his audience to say something about Denis. 'Ah! now,' he mused, a light gleaming in his eyes. 'Now we're talking about someone *different*.' Denis could pick up any old bat – someone else's as often as not – and make it sound like a Stradivarius. I dare say Victor Trumper had the same facility.

It was R. C. Robertson-Glasgow who wrote that Denis had genius but that if he was aware of the fact he didn't care. Neville Cardus observed that while most cricketers, even the greatest, need the evidence of the scoreboard to demonstrate their gifts, Denis fascinated all lovers of cricket, informed and uninformed, whether he was making runs or not. He was simply incapable of being anonymous. He could never, ever be boring.

My mind goes back to that halcyon summer of 1947 when the country was still down-at-heel and coping with the inevitable privations of the war's aftermath. We flocked to the cricket in our thousands, old delights to be savoured, and rejoiced as he and Bill Edrich held sway and Denis set two records that may never be surpassed. It was easy to feel then that God was in his heaven and that all was right with the world – a cricketer's at least.

The names of Compton and Edrich will be for ever remembered in any history of that era. For an appraisal of that happy and productive partnership I quote Jim Swanton, who has written that 'Compton as a cricketer was born great; Edrich achieved greatness, which was thrust upon him before he was quite ready to shoulder the burden.' It has been my only sadness in writing this book that I was unable to talk with Bill Edrich, a brave old friend who lived and ended his vibrant life in the fast lane. But we spoke often enough about Denis, and much of what I remember is set down in these pages.

In terms of technique and temperament, as I shall shortly seek to demonstrate, Denis had no obvious point of weakness. It might be claimed, indeed, that in attack or defence, on all pitches and in all conditions, he was better armed in his physical prime than any batsman since Jack Hobbs. He had the ability and, more importantly, the constant will to dominate. Alec Bedser is not alone amongst the great bowlers in saying that, once Denis got 'in', he found it harder to keep him quiet than any other England batsman he confronted.

No cause was lost until the last throw of the dice; nor was it for Edrich. Denis's courage and resolution in unnerving circumstances was never found wanting. He had a flexible, spontaneous, eternally boyish approach, and a natural, unforced modesty. He played for his team and not for himself – so unselfishly in fact that he was rarely what you would call a big score man; in this respect he had an affinity with Jack Hobbs.

An old Middlesex colleague, Harry Sharp, reckons that Denis's big innings were calculated according to the size of the crowd: 10 runs per thousand spectators. The big occasion got his adrenalin flowing and he rarely failed to come up trumps when playing in someone's benefit match. Sharp says, in the nicest possible way, that Denis could never quite understand why other people couldn't play like him. Some of the greatest performers in a variety of sports have been equally puzzled.

It can be no wonder that a cricketer of such style, with all the traits in his approach which I have sought to list – not to mention his footballing exploits with Arsenal and as a war-time international – should have become one of our greatest sporting heroes.

Only two England cricketers since Denis's time, Ted Dexter and Ian Botham, have had the same capacity to draw the crowds. Whereas Botham has thrilled and assaulted the senses, Denis simply captivated

2

an audience intrigued to know what might be the next pleasure in store, and which shared his obvious delight when it was revealed.

That magic quality, charisma, is difficult to define but we can all be conscious of its presence. Denis's fan club included boys from nine to ninety, and girls of every age. They all fell under the spell of a magnetic charm exerted without the slightest effort. It was an asset, as Fred Titmus attests, which unfailingly produced the desired result when the Middlesex players felt like seeing a show in the West End or in the provinces. 'It was always left to Denis to ring up the box office. The old magic never failed, home or away.'

*   *   *

It is easy to retain a memory of Denis as the eternally dashing cavalier yet, when the chips were down, the happy-go-lucky exterior masked an inward steel. Colin Cowdrey thinks he was a very stern competitor who always hated getting out – when it really mattered – and played everything, including golf and a variety of card games, to win. Joe Mercer attests to his combative approach at football.

On the cricket field Denis was always a traditionalist with an instinctive sense of the ethos of a game which has always demanded, *inter alia*, that a batsman departs from his crease without demur even though he feels or knows that the umpire has made a mistake. His old Middlesex colleague, Jack Young, says he never saw a player so quick to walk when the umpire's finger was raised. In an era when cricket at all levels was played with dignity, modesty and sportsmanship – and happily that mostly still applies – Denis was foremost in upholding the old essential values.

He was chivalrous, too. His dislike for putting the boot in when an opponent was down is illustrated by a story told by Ian Peebles. Not long after the war, Denis was confronted by a veteran county bowler, well past his best, who came on for a late spell, having suffered much punishment earlier in the day. Denis, by then in full spate, quietly played out a maiden over. His partner walked down the pitch to enquire why he had let up. 'Well,' Denis said, 'I thought the old boy looked just about all in.'

Rarely loath to tilt at windmills at the batting crease, Denis throughout his three score years and more has never been reluctant to take a gamble in other happy pursuits, notably the defeat of bookmakers. I don't think he has ever managed to put any of them out of business, but it has never been for the want of trying – or for lack of nerve in a crisis. Frank Tyson remembers him being hundreds of pounds down in Cape Town when it needed a very substantial outlay on the last, odds-on favourite to recoup his losses. Denis recouped.

Trevor Bailey recalls events at Sydney race course when Denis, towards the end of a losing afternoon, decided to put plenty on horse number nine in the last race. 'A helpful bookie told him he wanted seven, not nine, so Denis switched his bet. Number seven romped home and Denis collected a hundred quid. He'd rejoined the rest of the lads when the bookie charged up to say that he'd forgotten to pay him his stake money. So that was another tenner. Can you imagine it happening to anybody else? He had to be the Golden Boy. It was just the same at the bridge table; he always held good cards. Just as well he was a very bad player.'

On the shove ha'penny board, Denis and Jack Young, who hogged possession of it, were acknowledged as the Middlesex masters. When it came to playing poker, however, Denis was much less of an expert. He and Bill Edrich were involved in a brag party with some of the young players – the table piled with cash and cheques – when Gubby Allen entered the dressing room. The senior *duo* were berated for setting their juniors a poor example, and told to stop. This decision upset the young rookies more than it did the older pros. 'We were playing,' Alan Moss reflects, 'with the senior professionals' money.' John Murray has a similar memory. 'At poker,' he says, 'you could read Denis like a book.'

*　　　*　　　*

In writing a biography about an old friend one has greatly admired, it is no doubt necessary to guard against it becoming an unvarying litany of praise. This danger, I am sure, was in the mind of a well-meaning acquaintance who advised me not to forget the warts. I had to tell him that to the best of my knowledge, Denis has always been one of those lucky people without an enemy in the world. I am certainly prepared to say without fear of rebuttal that you will not come across any cricketer who played with or against Denis who has a harsh word to say about him. That is not to imply that he is a man without endearing weaknesses. Some of them have driven his friends to frustration.

He has never had much sense of time, he can be forgetful more often than not, and in spite of renewed endeavours to arrange his life more methodically, he has largely continued it in a thoroughly disorganized fashion. He has never, I think, carried his own personal diary and, being of an easy and accommodating temperament, has always found it difficult to say no to anybody. He might thus find himself booked for several contrasting engagements at the same time or, in the happy event of committing himself to just one of them, might get confused about time and venue.

This last frailty may explain how, when J. J. Warr retired from his financial eyrie in the City of London, Denis turned up at the Stock Exchange at 5.30 on a Tuesday afternoon when it was arranged for 4.30 at the Royal Exchange on the following day.

Denis's whole life has been strewn with examples of this sort, so those who know the form adhere to an eleventh commandment requiring them *never* to ask Denis to anything without first checking with his wife and/or secretary. This precaution having been taken in advance of an evening engagement, it would then be necessary to guard him throughout the day, with a pair of handcuffs available.

When explaining how he had come to arrive late for a function, or how he had failed to arrive at all, Denis might plead that one of his sisters-in-law, of whom there has been an apparently inexhaustible supply, had established a demanding claim on his presence at the eleventh hour. Whatever the excuse, it would be offered with quite disarming and irresistible charm.

The old magic persists. These days he has only to roll up at a sporting function on that groggy knee and everyone there, young and old, is conscious of the presence of a superstar wholly untouched by some of the excesses which fame can arouse. Les Vanter, his old sports editor on the *Sunday Express*, once got him to speak at the Beckenham rugby dinner – having chained him down at the Cricketers' Club off Baker Street throughout a convivial afternoon. 'He spoke entirely on cricket for half an hour, and simply held his audience in thrall.'

*   *   *

I cannot think of any cricketer to whom mere statistics or the accumu-

5

lation of runs meant so little, but none the less I must now set out some essential figures.

In a first-class career which began in 1936 and to all intents and purposes ended prematurely in 1957, he scored 38,942 runs, including 123 hundreds, at an average of 51.85. He made four appearances as an amateur in 1958 and subsequently went on unofficial tours to Transvaal and Jamaica before bowing out in Lancashire's centenary game against MCC in 1964.

In seventy-eight Test matches his aggregate was 5,807 runs, with seventeen hundreds, at an average of 50.06. He became, in 1938, the youngest cricketer to win an England cap and to make a Test century. Brian Close, at 18 years and 149 days, became (and remains) England's youngest Test cricketer when capped against New Zealand at Old Trafford in 1949. Denis, 20 years and 19 days, remains their youngest century-maker.

When he had played his last game for his country only Walter Hammond, Don Bradman and Len Hutton had scored more Test runs than him. Since then, in the English list alone, he has been overtaken by Geoffrey Boycott, Ken Barrington and David Gower, of whom the first and third named have played considerably more matches.

His name may for ever be associated with four records, three of which were established in 1947. In that English summer he scored the most runs (3,816) and the most hundreds (18) made in one season. He also – as may be less familiar – got a record number of runs (4,962) in one calendar year, with twenty-two hundreds and seventeen fifties in sixty-nine innings. This was progress which only Don Bradman – over his whole career – has matched. Denis also holds the record for the fastest triple hundred (300 in 181 minutes at Benoni in South Africa in 1948/49). Someone will need to hurry if that one is to be bettered.

It is important when looking at Denis's achievements in terms of figures alone to realize that his career spanned three distinct phases. First, the pre-war years to 1939, by which time he and Len Hutton were established as the two finest young batsmen of their generation, the cricket world apparently at their feet. Then came the peak years, 1946 to 1949, in which he made no fewer than 14,641 runs and fifty-nine hundreds. By the end of that period his Test average, 1937 to 1949, was exactly 58. He was 31 years of age, in his batting prime. The third and last phase covered the eight years 1950 to 1957 – exactly half of his career in English cricket – when he fought a constant and finally losing battle with his ailing knee. Whereas in his four golden years he had made twenty-eight championship hundreds for Middlesex, in his last eight seasons he managed no more than twenty-two. He was 39 when he retired from regular first-class cricket: an age when a richly talented batsman, still in good physical shape, might look forward to some more fruitful years. It was an age when Jack Hobbs had still to score his last ninety-eight centuries.

Batting Technique

DENIS WAS ENDOWED by nature with a robust frame, unusual strength in his forearms, an instinctive sense of balance and the gift given the greatest players of seeing the ball early. Yet to watch him walk out to bat one had the feeling that there was something a little ungainly. A slight roll in his gait led E. W. Swanton to remark that it was as though, when the construction of this 'creditable machine' was completed, no one thought to go round and give the nuts and bolts a final turn; some of the joints were a shade on the loose side.

Having taken guard on leg stump, twiddled his bat a time or two and surveyed the field, he settled into an easy, natural stance which an old purist might have faulted in only one minor particular: the left shoulder was pointed towards mid-on. His first movement to quicker bowlers was invariably back and slightly across his stumps to give himself more time, especially against the short-pitched ball. In this his technique differed from that of Len Hutton, who initially went half forward, or of Bill Edrich who pushed his front foot out rather more. Len Hutton, much influenced by Herbert Sutcliffe, used to get himself on the back foot in his early days but changed his style when the lbw law was changed in 1935. To give a decision in the bowler's favour before that date, an umpire had to satisfy himself that the ball had pitched in a straight line between the wickets. Now a batsman could be out to a ball which pitched on the offside of the stumps if the umpire considered that it would have hit the wicket, and if his body was in line between wicket and wicket.

From the outset of his career with Middlesex, Denis was urged by Patsy Hendren to use his crease. Patsy, incidentally, thought that Denis played as straight as any young player he had seen, his methods always basically correct. When Denis decided to play a stroke off the back foot, he used his crease so fully that Godfrey Evans, who ought to know about these things, wondered how he so rarely brushed the stumps. Colin Cowdrey always admired the way he manoeuvred the ball around. 'He watched the ball right on to the bat under his nose, *feeling* it so you were hardly aware of impact on the bat.'

Denis had all the known strokes at his disposal as well as several of his own contrivance. On the off side, his favoured area ran from fine third man to mid-off, on the leg side from mid-on to fine leg. This left an area on either side of the bowler which was rarely exploited but might certainly be explored when he put his mind to it, as various well-known stories have confirmed.

The most popular of these features Walter Robins who asked Denis, not out and in full spate by the tea interval, why no one had seen him play the straight drive. 'Right,' said Denis, 'watch the next over.' This did not quite satisfy his captain. 'I shall want evidence off the *third* ball.' 'Right,' said Denis yet again, whereupon the nominated ball disappeared into the members' enclosure behind the bowler's arm, put there by a stroke which would have satisfied the most pedantic critic.

There were three shots in Denis's armoury which I, and surely all those lucky enough to see him play, recall with special joy. One was the late cut which he employed, by no means always from within his crease, to great effect. He refined this stroke in 1947, playing it later and finer with impish delight and often, after advancing well down the pitch, using it at the last split second when a bowler, having seen him coming, pitched it short. No doubt in this age of in-slant and bowling aimed at the leg stump he would now find himself more restricted in the use of this shot, but I am certain that by giving himself room for it he would still find opportunities to tickle our taste buds.

He square cut mostly off his front foot, and it goes almost without saying that with his full use of the crease he was able to play, and *place*, the forcing back shots to quite a wide segment on the off side. Most of his driving, in the area of mid-off and extra cover, was done off his back foot. But what he could do in the direction of cover point was something not just different but unique.

When Denis played his cover drive the purist could say with truth that the left foot was rarely quite at the pitch of the ball, but he was never a theorist and he did what came naturally. In fact he deliberately left the gap between bat and pad as he executed this favourite stroke in order to give his potent shoulders and forearms more leverage. The result was that by playing the stroke a shade early or a shade late, he could place the ball precisely. The classicists can say what they like; it was very, very rare for Denis's cover drive to be played off anything but the middle of his bat.

There can never, I swear, have been a batsman who teased and frustrated cover points as much as Denis did. He brought his cover drive to a virtual peak of perfection in his most golden summer.

On the other side of the wicket Denis had total command of the drive or back foot force between long on and square leg, turning the wrist and using a strong bottom hand to control the direction of his strokes, and he was one of the finest and most controlled hookers of a cricket ball the game can have seen.

If a batsman can't hook effectively, it is better that he does not essay it, but to Denis, with his eye for a challenge and swift footwork, the shot was a telling weapon against fast bowlers. He had plenty of opportunities to use it when Ray Lindwall and Keith Miller were at their peak in 1948, although, in fact, he received fewer bouncers from that pair than Len Hutton, for whom the hook was not part of a repertoire complete in all other respects. Len, after his arm injury, discarded it on the grounds that it involved too much risk.

The essential thing about Denis's hook stroke, apart from the daring and spirit of counter-attack with which he played it, was its technical purity. His right foot was across and outside the line, so that he could play the ball down, one might say helping it safely round, on the leg side. Moreover he, like all of the finest players of his era, never, in helmetless days, took his eye off the ball. If its bounce was too high, he took evasive action rather than risk a top edge. To a ball rearing nastily from just short of a length he would go on to the back foot, with his nose right over the ball, to play it down with a dead bat.

If there was the merest chink in Denis's armour it might have lain in his leg-glance, a shot which gathered him many runs but very occasionally got him into trouble because he tended to move across his stumps a shade too far against the quickest bowling. The result in this case might be a catch for the wicketkeeper down the leg side.

Finally, to the third stroke which had us all purring with pleasure and wonder – the sweep. It is a dangerous shot for lesser mortals to attempt on the most reliable of surfaces, and even for Denis there could be a risk if the bounce was uneven. However, the stroke very rarely got him out and no one brought its execution to a finer art.

In playing this shot he was guided not by the direction of the ball but by its length. He pushed his front leg up the pitch and *swept* the blade of his bat, angled slightly down, across the line of the ball, thereby minimizing the chance of a top edge. He usually played the ball into the area between long leg and deep fine leg, but, by playing the shot earlier, he could also drive a deep square leg to the same frustration suffered by cover points. It is worth noting that despite his own talent for improvisation, Denis abhors the modern reverse sweep.

If all bowling might come alike to Denis at his best, it was the slow stuff that inspired him to provide us with many of our happiest moments. No one, I think, was quicker or more assured in his footwork, or more prepared to go down the pitch. We can forget the times when, against his natural instincts, he was advised by two cautious Test captains Hammond and Hutton to play the spinners from behind the crease. That was simply not his style.

It was a fortunate coincidence that in Patsy Hendren, an early and influential mentor, he should find someone with his own zestful approach. Patsy, of course, was one of the great hookers. He also had the footwork and the determination to play spin from down the pitch. Denis greatly admired the manner in which Patsy confronted 'Tich' Freeman, the Kent leg-spinner, and he himself needed very little encouragement to adopt the same methods. Walter Robins, who as Middlesex captain was able to get the very best out of Denis, consistently endorsed the way he played.

In his formative years as a pro he was told to watch the leg-spinner's wrist if he wanted to detect the wrong 'un but he came, like a few of the greatest players, to read the spin in the ball's flight. If he got it wrong, he would use his pad as a second line of defence. Freddie Brown, who purveyed leg-breaks and googlies for Cambridge, Surrey, Northants and England, found him a fascinating chap to bowl at. 'You always felt as a bowler that he was giving you a bit of a chance.'

In that respect, of course, he had to be a spur to all types of bowler; there was no dry-as-dust defence, the bad ball patiently awaited. In any case, as Trevor Bailey has observed, Denis had something in his locker which was shared by the finest players and consistently frustrated all bowlers: he could hit the *good* ball for four.

If Len Hutton was an even better player of orthodox left arm spin, I doubt whether you will find any of his contemporaries to dispute that Denis was a quite tremendous player of the off-break. Jim Laker, acknowledged master of his trade, could be amazed by Denis's capacity to make room on turning pitches and hit him with complete assurance on the off side. Another outstanding off-spinner, Tom Goddard of Gloucestershire, regularly suffered the same fate and was so utterly perplexed on one occasion that he admitted to his wicket keeper, Andy Wilson, 'I just don't know where to bowl at this young booger.'

Tom was not the only person worried; so was Andy. There is no more taxing job for a stumper than 'keeping to an off-spinner, especially on a turning pitch. In such circumstances Denis might be content to play Tom on the leg side from about a yard out of his crease and turn with the stroke – which meant that the wicket keeper got a sight of the ball, when it happened to defeat Denis, only at the last instant.

As to Denis's incomparable gifts for improvisation, I will leave one of them, which involved Tom Goddard, to a later chapter and quote here two examples which also stem from a Gloucestershire source. Bowling at him at Lord's in 1954, the off-spinner 'Bomber' Wells, one of the game's great characters, floated up a full toss leg-break round about middle and off. 'He was going like a train and he could have hit it anywhere in front of the wicket, but what did he do? He made room for himself and cut it for 4 *via the off bail*. Compton b Wells 82.'

On another occasion, at the old Wagon Works ground in Gloucester, 'Bomber' thought he had Denis's dismissal nicely worked out. Having tucked him up with several off-breaks just short of a length, he let go a quick outswinger which began its course just outside the leg stump. 'He was all set to play his sweep. Suddenly he shouts, "A swinger!" He changes his mind and he hits me for four, plonk off the middle of the bat, through the covers. It was the most astonishing shot I ever saw.'

Truly may Sir Leonard Hutton remark that Denis could play the correct game as well as anybody and the unorthodox one better than anyone he has ever seen. 'I wish,' he says, 'that I could have had a left arm as good as Denis's. This is the one that gives essential control, and Denis had the best one in the business.' It is a view reiterated by Jack Robertson, so often his batting partner for Middlesex. 'He had marvellous control with the top hand. And, when the chips were down, no one played straighter, no one was better in a crisis, even on bad pitches. He had the flair, the improvisation and the determination not to let any bowler call the tune.'

I must not omit to mention one more interesting observation about his technique by R. E. S. Wyatt, who is not only England's oldest surviving Test captain but now their most senior Test cricketer. 'Like all the best players he always kept his head still. When you do that, the camera doesn't wobble about.'

Other Activities

Between wickets

That renowned wit and after-dinner speaker, J. J. Warr (Cambridge University, Middlesex and England), has made some definitive judgements on Denis's calling and running between wickets. He never fails to have a sporting audience rolling in the aisles with his account of unfortunate mishaps between the wickets, while Peter Parfitt, another orator in much demand, has also made them part of his highly entertaining repertoire. The passage of time has ensured that everything has got exaggerated and Denis himself likes to add to the legend with an improbable claim that Bill Frindall has listed him as being involved in no fewer than 275 run-outs.

John Warr asserts that Denis is the only batsman in the history of the game to have called his partner for a single and to have wished him the best of luck at the same time. The first call, he goes on to say, was an opening bid, a tentative statement of policy. The second one was a basis for negotiation. So the sequence from the striker's end might go as follows, 'Yes . . . wait . . . no . . . oh! Christ . . . sorry!'

John also likes to relate the story of how he came out to join Denis on one of the very rare occasions when with all his knee troubles he allowed himself to have a runner. 'Don't worry, Compo, I'll play the shots,' he remembers saying. 'But in no time at all it was the only instance in the whole history of Lord's when both batsmen plus the runner all finished up at one end.'

Wisden has recorded that in 839 innings Denis was run out twenty-six times, which seems a modest percentage. What, of course, it does not and cannot reveal is how many of his partners suffered this fate, and what proportion of them had good reason to think it was not their fault. There can be no doubt that Denis was not consistently the best judge of a run and there might always be trouble when he set off for quick singles on the off side, having forgotten who was fielding at cover point. But I dare say that if we *did* know the unattainable statistics the figures would be rather less than commonly supposed.

Some very fine England players will tell you that Denis never ran them out, Joe Hardstaff, Sir Leonard Hutton, Cyril Washbrook, Reg Simpson, Peter May, Colin Cowdrey, Tom Graveney and Godfrey

Evans among them. Joe is emphatic that during the course of some good partnerships with Denis nothing approaching a run-out occurred. 'It was a joy to stand at the other end, and watch him play.'

Reg takes exactly the same line: 'You couldn't help but enjoy batting with him and, as for the other thing, if you were quick between the wickets and called and ran without hesitation, there were no problems.' 'We never had a tangle between the wickets,' Tom asserts. Godfrey says he and Denis always ran well together. 'I always went when he called me, even on the sixth ball – which was more than some might do.' Godfrey of course was as quick as anyone between wickets.

Cyril Washbrook takes a different stance: 'Running – apart from that knee – was just about his only problem. In the event of a mishap he was always full of apology to his unlucky partner. When batting with him I endeavoured to assume command of run selection in a loud and clear voice. I am certain it was the only way to survive.' So the evidence is conflicting.

Another England player who inclines to Washbrook's view is Trevor Bailey, who batted with Denis in a Test match against Pakistan at Old Trafford in 1954. 'I set off for a run when Denis called me,' Trevor remembers, 'and I was a third of the way down the pitch when he yelled "Wait!" Then he said "No" as we passed each other. So you might say I was a victim of the three-call trick.'

You may rightly suppose that England cricketers had fewer opportunities for disaster than Middlesex players, who batted with Denis far more often. The well known example at county level involves his elder brother Leslie, whose Benefit match was the Sussex fixture over the Whitsun holiday at Lord's – in the same season that Bailey had his unhappy experience. Denis managed to run out 'big Les' for 1, a notable achievement in the circumstances. At that late stage in his career Leslie, ever willing to indulge his younger brother's slightest whim, rumbled out of the starting block and stood not the slightest chance in response to Denis's ill-judged call.

Bill Edrich told me shortly before he died that during all the partnerships he had with Denis, the run-outs were never so many as generally thought. There is no denying, however, that they often got themselves into a tangle, more likely perhaps on the fifth or sixth ball of an over when both of them fancied retaining the strike.

I am certainly not implying by this that either of them ever ran selfishly when the needs of their partner or their side demanded otherwise. Jack Young, who thought Denis was a very bad judge of a run, says that Edrich never showed the slightest animosity after disaster had struck.

Apart from Bill, no one, I suppose, partnered Denis more often than Jack Robertson, who was one of those never to be run out by him. 'I took charge and said "No",' he recalls.'He was never selfish, simply a bad judge of a run. He did Alec Thompson five times in one season. Being a junior member of the side, Alec never argued over the wisdom of the call, but simply went.'

Alan Moss offers the theory that Jack, being deaf in his right ear, had to be a good partner for Denis, and would have been perfect if afflicted likewise in the other one. This frailty explains why relatively inexperienced wicket keepers thought Jack unsociable when he was batting; he simply could not hear what they were saying.

Fred Titmus echoes Thompson's attitude. 'Young players were nervous and, if he looked like coming, you went. You didn't want to run him out. Walter Robins wouldn't have been best pleased. But he was lovely to bat with; he took the pressure off you.' Don Bennett says much the same. He *was* run out once by Denis but admits that it was his own fault. 'I was only 16 at the time, and I marvelled how he could play like he did on one and a half knees.'

John Murray and Harry Sharp were other Middlesex players who always survived the worst, Harry alleging that all the stories about Denis's calling and running have been exaggerated, which is what I have suggested. Perhaps we may pay our money, and make our choice.

Bowling

If Denis's aggregate of 3,816 runs in the English season of 1947 is imprinted in the minds of anyone with a pretension to knowing his cricket history, I suspect that many of those who never saw Denis play are much less familiar with his all-round achievements. A young man collecting his *Wisdens* and *Playfairs* in the modern era will be able to tell you who scored the most runs and the most hundreds in a season, but ask him what else Denis achieved in his resplendent summer of 1947 and he may find the question taxing.

The answer is that he also captured 73 wickets. Indeed, in the four years from 1946 to 1949, inclusive of MCC tours to Australia, New Zealand and South Africa, he took 238 wickets to add to his remarkable aggregate of 14,641 runs and fifty-nine centuries.

Those were his most productive years as a bowler. From 1950 until the end of his career, while living with his knee problems, he mostly

15

bowled a good deal less but still contrived in 1952, a summer which left him unsatisfied as a batsman, to enjoy his most successful season in this respect. He then had 77 wickets, all but three of them for Middlesex, at an average of 28. In his last full season, 1957, his average of 24 – for 38 wickets – was the best he achieved in any summer at home.

In the pre-war years Denis was an orthodox slow left-arm bowler with a nice loop in his flight and a capacity to spin the ball on all but the blandest of surfaces. Those were not the days when bowlers of his type were encouraged to fire the ball in on the leg stump. Walter Robins, the Middlesex captain during Denis's first three summers, sometimes brought him on as third or fourth change to break up a partnership or to keep things orderly with command of line and length to an offside six-three field. The motivation for developing another style of bowling was, I think, first apparent in India during the war when Denis found his conventional methods unrewarding on the lifeless pitches there. He had also been impressed by the methods of the Australian Fleetwood-Smith in 1938. 'Chuck' Fleetwood-Smith was an unorthodox left-arm bowler with exceptional powers of spin.

Back home in 1946, he was experimenting at the nets with wrist spin out of the back of the hand. The stock ball was an off-break to the right-handed bat (the chinaman) and the wrong 'un went the other way. The Australian, Jack Walsh, who was currently the prime purveyor of this style in the English game, passed on some valuable guidance to someone who admitted that he had trouble in spotting his googly.

Walter Robins also encouraged Denis to persevere with new-found skills although in 1946, if Jack Young's standard slow left arm was failing to do the trick, the captain would still have Denis on in his original style. A transition to the new one was effected in 1947, and of course it suited him perfectly. Inevitably there were highs and lows but it was a challenge, it was unpredictable and above all, it was fun. He could still revert to the old style when conditions required it.

As it happened, the hard, dusting pitches in the second half of the 1947 summer gave him something to work on. A year later, in similar conditions at Headingley, he would surely have won a Test match against Australia with better support from his field. Even Don Bradman found his googly difficult to read. There could be no doubts about his powers of spin, and there could also be a disconcerting dip in the flight.

Godfrey Evans, England's wicket keeper at Headingley in 1948, says he never saw Denis bowl better than he did just before lunch on the final day; he thinks that as a bowler Denis rarely got the credit he deserved. Surrey's batsmen must have given him plenty however when, in August 1947, after scoring 137 not out, he ran through them twice to take twelve wickets. Sir Leonard Hutton considers that at times he was as good a bowler as Fleetwood-Smith, if not better, and wonders why he was not used more often. In fact Denis was only rarely employed as a bowler under Hutton's captaincy but it should be added that the era coincided with his all too familiar knee problems.

Denis took a total of 622 wickets during his first-class career, his most startling figures being those with which in his old orthodox fashion he dispatched Auckland on MCC's tour of New Zealand in 1946/47. He had seven for 46 and four for 13 after making 97 not out. This was one of three occasions when he took ten or more wickets in a match.

In the latter half of his career, and for some time afterwards, the 'funny stuff' was made to measure for relaxing, light-hearted affairs such as one recalled by John Warr. The Duke of Norfolk, batting at Arundel, had been assisted by the fielding side to 20-odd, at which point it was thought that charity had gone far enough. 'Brought on for the execution, Denis pitched a perfect googly on the leg peg which was smashed over extra cover for 6. The Duke was perplexed when the entire fielding side fell about laughing.'

Fielding

In his physical prime, fleet of foot and possessed of a very strong left arm, Denis could field with distinction anywhere. At leg slip to pace bowlers – there is an echo here of Ian Botham's method on the other side of the wicket – he would stand much closer to the bat than ordinary mortals and by so doing accept more chances. On tour in South Africa in 1948/49 he held 24 catches, many of them at silly mid-off to Roly Jenkins or Jack Young, and apparently never missed a thing. John Warr has always held that Denis was capable of catching anything provided that he happened to be looking at the time!

There were times, certainly, when his attention was allowed to wander. He could be bored by dull batting. He enjoyed a good gossip with fellow fielders or, if he was stationed in the outfield, with spectators. In his first Test match he was reproved by his captain, Walter Robins, for keeping his hands on his knees in the gully – a lapse from convention that may only inhibit lesser players. On another occasion, after he had missed a very difficult swirling catch in the outfield, with the sun in his

17

eyes, he was told by Robins to go off and get a cap, and not chat up the paying customers.

Ian Peebles has recalled a moment during the Sussex–Middlesex game at Hove during the August Bank Holiday in 1938. 'I can still see John Langridge pushing forward, and edging the ball gently straight to first slip. First slip, regrettably, was in the midst of a beautiful reverie, and somewhat startled to receive the intrusive ball smack in the navel. The point of the tale is the deportment of the offender in the face of the dual stream of vituperation which proceeded from captain and bowler. So good natured and apologetic was he that one felt almost ashamed, a most unheard of state of mind for a bowler deprived of his prey.'

On his first tour of South Africa, in 1948/49, Alec Bedser was in the middle of his run-up at the start of a Test match when the captain, George Mann, noticed his slip tying up a boot lace. 'Should I stop Alec from bowling?' Mann considered. 'I decided that when in doubt, do nothing. Denis, attending to the final knot, still had no trouble in making the catch look easy. Yet another example of disorganization and flair.'

Eight years later, when England took the field at Johannesburg at the start of another series against South Africa, Peter May thought it prudent, because of Denis's inflexible knee, to station him at long leg. Moving ever nearer to the wicket as Brian Statham bowled the first over, Denis eventually arrived in a close catching position, there to be spotted by an irate captain.

'What the hell are you doing there, Compo?'
'I thought you'd need a bit of help close in.'
'Oh! my God, stay where you are and keep quiet.'

By then, sadly, Denis had got to a stage where for the close-in chances eye and hand remained in good alliance but the knee might not allow him lift-off. He could still cope, somehow or other, with the batting but it sickened him that he could not deliver the old goods in other ways.

Captaincy

In the seasons of 1951 and 1952, when Walter Robins could no longer spare the time to lead the Middlesex side, the county committee, for reasons best known to themselves, decreed that Denis and Bill Edrich should share the captaincy. Denis had enjoyed a taste of leadership when be became the first England cricket professional to be appointed vice-captain on an MCC tour to Australia, under Freddie Brown, in

1950/51. The Middlesex compromise, however, was not a success. Bill Edrich was appointed sole captain, and held the job until he retired from full-time playing at the end of the 1957 summer. J. J. Warr then took over.

If Denis's old colleagues are to be believed, and I dare say that distance lends enchantment and exaggeration to the view, the joint captaincy was such a rough and ready arrangement that the toss would be conducted by the one who arrived on the ground first. There are no prizes for guessing who turned up second, and there should be no surprise that on those occasions when he got there first matters might be subsequently conducted in a happily disorganized fashion.

The fact is that Denis was not cast by nature in a captain's role; he found it difficult to summon to the task the concentration that governed his batting when the chips were down. Of his occasional leadership in Australia on the 1950/51 tour Trevor Bailey reports that he really had very little idea of what was required. 'It was dire. His judgement was poor.' Jack Robertson thinks his captaincy of Middlesex was a disaster. 'Matches were simply allowed to drift, and that came as a big contrast after we'd had Walter Robins simply telling us to play while he conducted the orchestra.'

Asked briefly to describe Denis's captaincy, Jack Young ventures the epithet 'terrible' and Alan Moss another, 'impossible'. Fred Titmus reckons he was lucky to have missed playing under Denis on account of doing his National Service. Don Bennett asserts that if Denis had continued as skipper, 'at least we wouldn't have had many draws'. I should add that all these uncomplimentary verdicts are made with a kindly, nostalgic twinkle in the eye.

Early Days

DENIS CHARLES SCOTT COMPTON was born at 20 Alexandra Road, Hendon, on May 23 1918 – the third and youngest member of his family, a brother for Leslie and Hilda. His parents, Harry and Jessie, who hailed from an Essex family, had moved to London where his father found more promising opportunities to run his own painting and decorating business.

Harry Compton was an enthusiastic and very useful club cricketer who captained the Old Boys' team of Bell Lane School in Hendon which both of his sons were to attend in due course. It seemed the natural thing for them to play cricket and football, much of it outside in their own street, as soon as they were old enough to do so without adult supervision.

When they got older still, a number 13 bus was not far away to convey them down the Finchley Road to their Mecca in London NW8 – Lord's – for the modest outlay of a penny or two.

Their sister Hilda, the middle member of the family, now 75, was also a natural athlete, who had represented England Schoolgirls in the 100 yards sprint.

Allowed at quite a tender age to accompany his father on his cricketing travels, Denis eventually occupied the position of scorer for the Bell Lane Old Boys and was thrilled to play as a late substitute if anyone had dropped out. E. W. Swanton has recalled how on one occasion the opposing side protested on the grounds that he was far too small and clearly they dare not bowl at him properly. Father Harry told them they could bowl as fast as they liked, which they did while a stripling of 12 with precocious talent made 40 or thereabouts.

When he went to Bell Lane School, Denis was fortunate to come under the influence of a stern but benevolent senior master, Mark Mitchell, who insisted on firm discipline, kept noses to the grindstone and reinforced the strongly traditional happy attitudes held by his parents. All this in his early years helped to ensure that a lad with a carefree, resilient nature would go through life upholding the old traditional standards of behaviour.

Mr Mitchell quickly discovered that Denis was not of an especially academic bent. Ian Peebles has told us that this master once asked Denis the question, 'If there were six posts in a row, how many spaces would there be between them?' 'Six,' Denis said. Mr Mitchell put down his book, more in sorrow than in anger. 'Compton,' he said, 'I will tell you now you will *never* be a scholar.' The master was to retain great interest in his pupil's later career, went frequently to Lord's to see him play and later, in the *Sunday Express*, was able to read Denis's regular articles and note to what extent his literary instructions had borne fruit.

In 1930, aged 12, and now captain of his school at cricket and football, Denis made 88 for North London Schools against South London Schools on a pitch close to the Tavern, his first innings on hallowed turf.

Two summers later, on the same ground, he had another, more significant chance to prove his mettle.

In mid-September 1932, shortly before Douglas Jardine's side sailed for Australia and a tour that rocked the cricket world, Denis was chosen as captain of London's Elementary Schools against Mr C. F. Tufnell's XI in an afternoon match at Lord's which was to have the most profound influence on his future. He shared an opening stand of exactly 100 with a lad from South London, A. J. McIntyre, who was run out for 42. With much aplomb young Denis went on to make 114 out of a total of 204 for eight declared.

The opposing side, captained by Desmond Eagar, a future leader of Hampshire, were bowled out for 56, Denis putting himself on as fourth change and acquiring the presentable analysis of two for 5 in four overs. His performance in this match earned him a 'Jack Hobbs' bat from the *Star* evening newspaper, and he soon had the joy of having the great man sign it himself.

Many years later Desmond Eagar wrote a letter to E. W. Swanton in which he said that he still remembered the occasion most vividly although 'it almost depressed me at the time to think that anyone could be so good as Denis at the same age as myself'.

The South London batsman previously mentioned, A. J. McIntyre, later of Surrey and England, has not forgotten that day either. 'Denis played a ball straight at cover, followed by "Yes" and then "No" and there I was, stranded in the middle of the pitch.' He adds that he subsequently made sure that Denis never ran him out again, although subsequent opportunities must roughly have been limited to the tour of Australia they made together in 1950/51. One might suggest that Arthur became Denis's first recorded run-out victim.

For Denis, however, this match was a momentous occasion because his innings was watched by several discerning people, among them Sir Pelham Warner, who not only knew an outstanding young cricketer when he saw one, but at that time exerted a profound influence on the game. So far as the Lord's ground staff was concerned – as one of its older surviving members has noted – if Sir Pelham thought you were good, you were half way there; if he thought otherwise, you might just as well have got a job as a bus conductor.

Denis's success in this match led directly to an offer from MCC to join its ground staff at the start of the following season. Understandably the offer was greeted with enthusiasm by Denis, and was warmly supported by his father. But his mother had some initial reservations. The life of a professional cricketer was an insecure one. Would not a steady job at Hendon Town Hall, or some such, offer more enduring prospects? Before long however she had to concede that she was fighting a losing battle, especially after Denis's talent on the football field caught the attention of Arsenal's management, and the possibility of a year-round career as a professional sportsman became likely.

Denis's brother Leslie was already on Arsenal's books and the Highbury scouts were aware of the exploits of his younger brother. Denis had played at left half for an England Schoolboys side against Wales in 1931 and he had been chosen for the England side in a trial at Chesterfield but, named as a reserve for the international against Scotland, he missed his Schoolboy's cap.

Arsenal's great manager, Herbert Chapman, stepped in with the suggestion that Denis should spend his winter months at Highbury. Thus everything was decided, and his mother was comforted that a year-round income would be assured.

Denis was interviewed at Lord's by the MCC Secretary, 'Billy' Findlay, who had kept wicket for Oxford and Lancashire in earlier days. The young man was made to feel at ease, and it was proposed that he should receive the going rate of twenty-five shillings a week. Neither then, nor ever afterwards, did he feel disposed to argue the toss about money. It always seemed to him a privilege simply to get paid to play a lovely game.

So in April 1933 young Denis, still some weeks short of his 15th birthday, joined MCC's ground staff fourth class by reporting himself to Phil Edwards, an amiable little man known as 'number one boy', who took his orders from the head groundsman, Harry White. The head groundsman lived in a cottage – which these days has become the MCC shop behind the new Mound Stand – with an immaculate kitchen garden and some Rhode Island Reds to keep him supplied with vegetables and eggs.

Staff members at the lower end of the pecking order like Denis were required to present themselves at 8 a.m. They would then be detailed off to undertake essential chores such as rolling the square, sweeping bird droppings off the seats and generally keeping the ground spick and span. During matches Denis was sometimes told to help in the scorebox, a job he greatly enjoyed since it involved watching what was going on out in the middle. Players like Hobbs, Hendren, Sutcliffe, Hammond and Woolley were some of the great batsmen to be seen.

There was another regular activity on match days which enabled him to see some cricket and also produced a handy financial bonus – selling match cards. From every match card sold at two pence each, one ha'penny would be deducted and put into a pool for all the groundstaff to share. Denis remembers that by the end of the Test match against Australia in 1934 he and all the lads shared almost £15, which was quite a rich picking in those days.

The second, third and fourth classes on the ground staff were housed on the upper floor of the building topped by the clock tower, which still stands at the Nursery end at Lord's. At the close of an innings a shout from below would summon the lads out to roll the pitch. These days on the upper floor there is a members' bar. The first class professional staff occupied a dressing room on – as you look at the pavilion from the front – the right hand side, next to what is now the Warner Stand.

The amateurs made their entrances to the field through a central gate – as all players do nowadays – after making their way down from one of two team dressing rooms on the first floor. There was a separate gate for the professional players to make their exits and their entrances. It was an upstairs downstairs era in which Andy Wilson, the old Gloucestershire wicketkeeper/batsman, reckons Lord's was a good and happy place to be.

Andy was a first class pro when Denis was serving his apprenticeship. He has recalled in *The Cricketer International* how the pros, before the Warner stand was built, would sit on a grassy bank in the evenings waiting for the stockbrokers and other city gents to turn up for a net. The telephone would ring in the No. 1 professionals' room: 'Mr Jones would like two bowlers, please.' MCC was, and remains, a private club, and its members are *still* entitled to their privileges.

When assembled and waiting for custom, the older pros were never above pulling rank by making sure they got the best payers. The quality of pay, not play, was a matter of some importance, and those members good for a five bob touch were quickly sorted out. The younger pros

23

would be left occasionally with members, known locally as 'stumors', who did not pay at all. They soon learned.

Denis was to enjoy one particular stroke of luck: he was invited to bowl at C. Aubrey Smith (not then knighted) whose portrayal of English gentlemen in Hollywood films had made him a worldwide reputation. After this, whenever he came back to Lord's he always asked for 'young Compton'. He regularly produced five bob, and was kind enough to sign his autograph. Denis rated 'Round the Corner' Smith as a fine player of the old school who liked to get on the front foot against all styles of bowling.

Discipline, Andy Wilson recalls, was basic and firmly though benignly enforced by the head coach and older pros; if you didn't behave, you didn't play; if you played and misbehaved, you were out. But in those days professionals unable to make the grade in county cricket were kept on at Lord's until MCC had found them a good coaching job elsewhere, mostly in public schools.

Practice for the young pros was organized on two afternoons a week, Denis first coming under the knowing eye of the head coach, George Fenner from Kent, who was soon to be succeeded by Archie Fowler. Fenner was a fine coach and a just disciplinarian who never sought to restrict a young batsman's favourite or most effective shots; he encouraged them to use their initiative and approved of Denis's sweep. When someone congratulated him on Denis's later success he said, 'I shouldn't say I coached him. Let's just say I didn't spoil him.'

Archie Fowler, a thick-set, kindly man who never shouted at anybody, was a mentor in the same mould. Denis thought him the best bowling coach a batsman might hope to practise with in the pre-war years. Archie would persist with great accuracy on the same line and length until both he and his pupil were satisfied. He told Denis not to listen to those who urged him to get his front foot closer to the pitch of the ball outside his off stump. Denis was never asked to read coaching manuals but left to develop those naturally attacking skills he had first revealed in a Hendon street and at school. On Sundays he developed them further by playing matches for his father's side or for Stamford Hill.

However, despite the latitude they gave Denis, both Archie Fowler and George Fenner insisted on certain basic tenets of defence. Even the greatest players such as Jack Hobbs and Patsy Hendren, Denis's two biggest heroes, had to defend. So of course did Walter Hammond, who had fired young Denis's ambitions with a splendid hundred at Lord's.

'I'd love one day to play with *him*,' Denis said to his coach. 'Work hard, my lad,' Archie replied, 'and one day you will.'

Jack Young, later to become a Middlesex and England slow left-arm bowler, was five years older than Denis when he first bowled at him in the nets at Lord's, not long after Denis had changed from short trousers into long cricket flannels. 'George Fenner told me just to bowl,' Jack says, 'and not to tell him anything. It was quite extraordinary. Even then he had an enormous *awareness*.'

Jack recalls a game not long afterwards, when Denis, looking like a young pixie, got 40-odd against a strong Indian Gymkhana side and astonished everyone with his maturity. And he remembers that Gubby Allen, lately returned from the Bodyline tour of Australia, would watch approvingly from behind the nets. No player gave Denis more consistent encouragement than Gubby did in the formative years.

According to Colin Cowdrey, who I think got the story from Patsy Hendren, 1934 may well have been the year when young Denis came up against Arthur Wellard, a Somerset and (later) England bowler, then in his prime, in a practice match at the Nursery end at Lord's. 'Wellard was told to have no fears about giving the lad the gun. He fired off five consecutive good length balls on the off stump which were hit off the middle of the bat to five different parts of the field.'

Also in 1934, his second summer at Lord's, Denis was selected for several MCC out matches against clubs or schools. One of these was a fixture at Beaumont College which may well have marked the first occasion when he played in the same side as Bill Edrich, his great partner who had recently arrived from Norfolk for a trial with Middlesex. MCC's captain, the author Alec Waugh, asked the pair of them what they did and, being told that they bowled, put Denis in at number 10 and Bill at 11. There was a splendid, much needed rearguard action for the last wicket.

For another MCC match, against Suffolk, Denis arrived in Felixstowe having left his cricket bag at Lord's. George Brown, an old Hampshire and England cricketer of much versatility, came to the rescue with flannels and boots but, since he stood some six inches taller than Denis, and had much bigger feet, the results were bizarre. Denis stuffed the boots with paper and, marching out to bat in baggy pants like a clown at the circus, could be forgiven for making 0. By the second day, and by his second innings, his own gear had arrived and he scored 110 with no trouble at all. He was certainly making an early mark.

Jack Robertson, who was on the Middlesex staff (and a year older than Denis), had his first partnership with him in 1934. Both of them got 50s for Chiswick Priory, a wandering side whom they played for occasionally, at West Drayton. 'Compo's maturity was astonishing,' Jack reflects. 'I hadn't the slightest doubt that he would play for England.'

For a while yet, however, these two future England players were obliged to pull the heavy roller on the Lord's square along with several others on the staff who were to make a name for themselves, notably Bill Edrich, Sid Brown, Harry Sharp, Laurie Gray and Alec Thompson. This work had its advantages; when they went out to bat there they knew every blade of grass.

In 1935 Denis played for the Young Professionals, captained by Andy Wilson, against Young Amateurs. Although he did not make a significant score, he impressed his skipper by the way he got his runs. 'He was obviously someone quite apart – and he had a good, long spell of accurate left-arm spin.' Later that summer Andy was senior pro when MCC toured the Channel Islands. 'He got good runs in Jersey and Guernsey with *my* bat and *my* socks.'

In the same summer, Denis, by then promoted to third class status on the staff, was chosen three times to play for Middlesex 2nd XI, but accomplished nothing out of the ordinary, his top score being only 12. On another occasion he was even asked to go with the 1st XI to Maidstone, but he was left out of the side in favour of Jack Young, after the pitch had been examined. But his next appearance in the Minor Counties Championship the following season was to lead to something a good deal more exciting.

1936: First Season for Middlesex

Accoording to gubby allen, Walter Robins, captain of Middlesex, although very rarely seen at net practice, was persuaded to take a close look at a precocious talent before the 1936 season got under way. Allen says that come April he was having a net at Lord's on four evenings a week, and always enjoyed bowling against the best young batsmen on the staff. Having found that against Compton he needed to slip himself a bit, he recommended that Robins ought to assess this young batsman's skills against top class spin bowling. So the Middlesex captain came down to the Nursery end to give Denis a new examination. Although Robins was a big spinner of the ball, and his googly was never easy to read, Denis seemed always to be in the right position for the right stroke and passed his test with much credit.

Towards the end of May 1936, just after his 18th birthday, Denis was chosen to play for Middlesex 2nd XI against Kent 2nd in a Minor Counties fixture at Folkestone. So also was E. W. Swanton, who went in first and was still at the crease after four wickets had fallen cheaply on a greenish pitch. Let Jim now take up the story.

'At this point there entered a juvenile figure with an oddly relaxed way of walking, somewhat loose round the knees and with a swaying of the shoulders, inclined to let his bat trail after him rather than use it as a stick in the usual fashion. As he had to pass me I thought a word of encouragement would not be out of place, and murmured something about playing up and down the line and there being nothing to worry about. My new companion thanked me politely, and very soon started pushing the ball round the field with every appearance of ease, and running up and down the pitch rather more quickly than his ponderous partner found comfortable. To within a run or two a hundred were put on for the fifth wicket, each of us just missing his fifty.'

Jim Swanton returned to Lord's and when asked by Robins whether anyone had distinguished himself simply said that he had been playing with the best young cricketer he had ever seen. Another shrewd observer, equally impressed, was the old Middlesex professional Jack Durston, who, on the eve of the Folkestone game, had told Denis that he was to stay in the team's hotel and not go to the local dance hall. What was more, Durston instructed Jack Young, the left-arm spinner, to make sure he kept Denis locked up.

27

It so happened that Middlesex found themselves a man short for the match against Sussex at Lord's, when the amateur George Newman had to withdraw from their side. Durston had also come back from Folkestone to sing Denis's praises to the Middlesex senior pro, Patsy Hendren, who, Young tells me, thought him still too young and inexperienced. The coach, Archie Fowler, also thought that Denis should be left alone while he developed his skills.

However, Gubby Allen had no doubts when the Middlesex skipper asked for his advice. Less than a month after his batting trial with Walter Robins Denis was chosen to make his first-class debut. After Jack Durston gave Denis the great news in the dressing room, a hurried telephone call was made to ensure that the Compton family attended the Whitsuntide fixture in force.

Sussex batted first to make 185, Denis first getting his name on the scoresheet by catching Parks, J.H., off the bowling of 'Big Jim' Smith. In the following season, Jim Parks Sr (father of the England wicket keeper/batsman) was to make 3,003 runs and take 101 wickets, a record which it is probably safe to say will never be surpassed. Later in the Sussex innings Denis captured his first wicket, that of Parks, H.W., brother of J.H., caught by Gubby Allen. Allen was fielding at mid-on and, upon seeing Jim Smith in a state of dither under a steeper destined to land in the mid-off area, ran across to hold a catch which he says was one of the best he ever made. At this time Denis was still bowling his orthodox slow left-arm spin.

When Middlesex went in to bat they had some early troubles against Maurice Tate who celebrated his 41st birthday by disposing of Hart, Hendren and Hulme, the Arsenal and England footballer, in one over. With his big feet splayed out to an angle of 45 degrees, Tate, one of cricket's greatest medium-fast bowlers, could still arch his back and summon up some of the old fire with his glorious action. Denis, who was down to go in at number 10, must have wondered whether his innings might be coming sooner rather than later. But the middle order battled away and eventually, when a first innings lead lay in the balance, Jim Smith was promoted above Denis and thrashed a rapid 28. So Denis went in last, at 1.15 p.m. on the second day, to join Gubby Allen, who was batting at number 9 after dislocating a finger.

To one as young as Denis, Allen was a figure demanding due reverence, as indeed was Tate, who was kind enough to wish the incoming batsman good luck, but no favours, as he approached the crease. 'Whatever else,' Allen said, 'play forward. He comes off the pitch much faster than you expect.' 'Yes, sir,' replied Denis, who promptly played back to a good length ball which whistled over the off stump.

After doing it again, with the same result, Denis now got the message, thrust his front foot forward and was soon at ease. He and Allen came safely through to lunch, Middlesex got their lead and the partnership produced 36 runs before Denis was given out lbw to Parks, J.H., for a highly creditable 14. The ball looked to have pitched outside the leg stump, and to have hit Denis's front pad rather high.

As the players left the field, Gubby Allen suggested to the umpire, Bill Bestwick, that it had not been one of his best decisions. He knew him well, so felt entitled to make such a mild observation, though he later regretted it. Bestwick said nothing then, but, when the fielding side re-emerged, he remarked to Allen, 'You were absolutely right, but that young chap is going to be a good player. I'd had too much beer at lunch and I was dying for a pee.' 'Good?' Gubby replied, 'he's going to be a damn sight better than that.'

In his biography of Denis, Ian Peebles remarked that he must have been the only number 11, in his first match, to be commended in *Wisden* for his batting. Denis did not go in again but his captain gave him a further chance with the ball in Sussex's second innings. He had Alan Melville, a future captain of South Africa, caught behind for 42. Two wickets in the match for 35 in fourteen overs was nothing to be ashamed about.

This opportune performance earned Denis selection in the next Middlesex game against Nottinghamshire at Lord's. Denis got 26 not out and 14 against Notts, and had the nerve to hook Harold Larwood for three fours. After this match he was never left out of the Middlesex side again except for injuries, representative calls or the occasional claims of Arsenal. The next few matches built upon his early season results. Although he got his first duck at first-class level against Northamptonshire, caught off the fiery 'Nobby' Clark, he more than made up for it with a fine 87 in the second innings.

At one point Middlesex had collapsed against Clark on a green pitch to 21 for five, but despite this Denis soon got into his stride, driving successive balls past cover for four. 'You know what's coming next?' his captain said. 'No,' came a naive reply. 'He'll let you have the bouncer,' Robins added. 'Well, if he does,' Denis said, 'I'll hook him.' Which he did, more than once, to great effect.

This has been E. W. Swanton's story so far; now for one from Ian Peebles, who told how Walter Robins kidded Clark by suggesting that if he went on expending such energy bowling to Denis he might be a lame duck by the time England came to choose their next touring side for Australia. Nobby was so impressed by the logic that he got his captain to take him off, whereupon Robins and Denis carried their partnership to 139 and Middlesex won with some ease.

That both these games were low-scoring affairs lent a greater sheen to Denis's effort as was the next against Yorkshire at Lord's in which he scored a composed 26 before being bowled by Hedley Verity. His next significant achievement came in the match against Northants at Northampton in which he registered his maiden first-class century, 100 not out. Of the 74 added for the last wicket with Ian Peebles, Denis made 56; he always enjoyed taking charge of last-ditch operations. 'By perfect timing,' *Wisden* reported, 'Compton drove, cut and pulled with remarkable power, and took out his bat, with fourteen 4s as his best strokes, in one and three-quarter hours.' He set himself a tempo for his first hundred which in most circumstances was to become more or less the norm.

His form for the rest of the season was inconsistent. 35 and 81 against Gloucestershire, an 80 in the return game with Sussex at Hove, and 77, in only seventy-five minutes, against Hampshire at Lord's were highlights. But his best performance of the season was to make 87 and 96, top score in both innings, against Kent at Maidstone. Not in the least disturbed by the reputation of Tich Freeman, the now veteran leg-spinner, he tackled him with such confidence that each innings was made in less than two hours.

He ended this summer with an aggregate of 1,004 first-class runs at an average of 34. He was awarded his county cap and promoted from third class to first on the Lord's staff. In championship games he stood second among the regular Middlesex batsmen to Hendren, who scored eight of the side's fifteen hundreds and more than a thousand runs in August alone. The county rose from third to second place in the championship, the title going to Derbyshire for the first and only time in their history.

Wisden observed that the leap into prominence of Denis Compton in 1936 was perhaps of greater significance than the continued excellence of Hendren. Their praise was supplemented by that of Sir Pelham Warner who described him at the end of that season as 'the best young batsman who has come out since Walter Hammond was a boy'.

Denis's first full season could have been even more rewarding. The MCC team to tour Australia in the winter of 1936/37 was chosen in

August. There was a considerable measure of support in committee for Denis's inclusion but the captain, Gubby Allen, felt that to send out a young cricketer so inexperienced entailed too much risk. 'I think,' Gubby reflects now, 'that if I'd said yes he would have gone. Who knows what might have happened if he had? It might have brought him on – or set him back.' With Test cricket interrupted by World War Two, it was to be ten years before Denis, at the age of 28, made his first tour of Australia.

1937: Debut for England

1937 WAS THE first full season that Denis played for Middlesex. It was a momentous one for himself and for his county. It marked the retirement of Patsy Hendren, one of the most popular players who ever graced the game; his 170 hundreds have been exceeded only by Jack Hobbs, his 57,611 runs surpassed only by Hobbs and Frank Woolley. Hendren, then in his 49th year, got five hundreds in his last thirteen innings to finish his career in a blaze of glory. The season also signalled the regular presence of Norfolk's Bill Edrich, now qualified to play for his new side. So while Middlesex said farewell to the survivor of one distinguished, long-serving duo, Hendren and J.W. ('Young Jack') Hearne, they could introduce another famous alliance which was to do them equally proud.

In 1937 Denis became, at 19 years and 84 days, the youngest cricketer to be chosen for England. He scored 1,980 runs, with three hundreds, at an average of 47, while Edrich, in seven more innings, got 2,154 at three runs less. In the early 1930s, when Middlesex were an ordinary side, their batting had been carried by Hendren. Things were different now, a transformation having begun when Walter Robins took over the captaincy in 1935 with his restless, energetic, up-and-at-'em approach. In 1937, moreover, Jim Sims and Jim Smith between them took more than 200 championship wickets, and Robins in all first-class matches missed the double by just one wicket.

After giving Yorkshire an excellent run for their money throughout most of the season, Middlesex faded in the final straight to finish second – a position that was to become increasingly familiar to them in the years ahead.

Apart from getting 41 and 54 in his first match of the summer, for MCC against Yorkshire, and 57 for Middlesex against Northants, Denis achieved little of any note until the latter half of May. He was then offered his first big representative opportunity: selection for the South side against the North in a Test trial at Lord's which formed part of the 150th anniversary celebrations of MCC. Walter Hammond dominated affairs by making 86 and 100 not out, but a new guard of outstandingly promising batsmen made their presence felt. Joe Hardstaff (Nottinghamshire), who had toured Australia the previous winter, got 71 while

Len Hutton's 102 must have booked him a place in the first Test match shortly to be played against New Zealand.

Denis, with 70 and 14 not out, thought it a privilege to observe Hammond at close quarters. The quality of his own display, rated as being second only to that of the master, could not have escaped the notice of England's selectors. Denis approached a fruitful month of June with 87 for Middlesex against Essex and, enjoying himself at the expense of the University bowlers on behalf of MCC, with 80 and 85 against Cambridge, and 116 and 50 against Oxford. He wasted little time in making that hundred. H. G. ('Tuppy') Owen-Smith got a yet more rapid 168 not out. 'Tuppy' was a great games player who had made a hundred before lunch for South Africa in the Headingley Test match of 1929. I saw him play full-back for England when they had their famous win over New Zealand at Twickenham in January 1936.

The New Zealanders were not a strong side, their bowling being heavily dependent on Jack Cowie, fast medium, whose ability to deliver the outswinger, and to bring the ball back off the pitch, stamped him as a performer in world class. He finished his tour with 114 first-class wickets; in the three Test matches, all played over three days, his haul of 19 at an average of 20 was more than twice as many as that of anyone else on either side. On the batting front, 'Curly' Page's team included three excellent young players, Walter Hadlee, Mervyn Wallace and Martin Donnelly, of whom the last named looked to be a rising star.

England ran out of time at Lord's after making 424 in their first innings with hundreds by Hardstaff and Hammond, and declaring in their second one at 226 for four. New Zealand scored 295 and 175 for eight. Len Hutton, falling twice to Cowie, made an inauspicious first appearance with 0 and 1, but was able to put things right at the first available opportunity.

That occurred in the second Test, at Old Trafford, where Len got exactly 100 in the first innings and England won by 130 runs. New Zealand may have paid a steep price for dropping Freddie Brown four times during a rumbustious 57 struck at a critical time in England's second innings. After that, Tom Goddard made short work of the opposition by taking six wickets for 29. Cowie had ten in the match for 140.

Back now, if briefly, to Denis's progress with Middlesex for whom he was to score consistently during the second half of the season. He batted once in their matches against Northants, Yorkshire and Lancashire, making 59, 45 and 63, and was then chosen for his first

Gentlemen–Players fixture. He got 0 and 34 not out for the winning side, being stumped off Freddie Brown in his first innings – which suggests an onrush of early zeal. This was by way of prelude to what surely was the first of his great innings.

When Gloucestershire came to Lord's he simply put their bowling to the sword in making 177 out of 279 in three hours. He revealed an early liking for the off-spin of Tom Goddard but no bowler suffered more than the amateur, Mr C. Tyler, whose military medium had surprisingly acquired five wickets for 37 before Denis ran amok. Walter Hammond, in close attendance at slip, must have been an impressed observer. He had noted Denis's promise in 1936. This innings was sure proof of a very special talent.

The bit now between his teeth, Denis next made 80 not out against Worcestershire at Lord's. The second innings occupied him for just forty-three minutes, so he was well on course for the fastest hundred of the season when his captain had to declare.

Not long afterwards he had the joy of watching Patsy Hendren get his first hundred of the summer, 187 against Sussex at Hove, and was happy enough to play second fiddle with 61 while his old mentor orchestrated affairs in a stand of 158.

A week later he got two modest scores against Surrey at The Oval but his spirits were uplifted by the news that he had been chosen to play for England in the third Test match against New Zealand. Before that Middlesex had to play Essex, against whom he was rarely to fail. Scores of 55 and 71 at Chelmsford sent him back rejoicing to Surrey's headquarters.

The last Test of the summer also marked the England debut of Cyril Washbrook, aged 22, who was called up to replace his unfit Lancashire colleague, Eddie Paynter. Rain permitted little more than half an hour's play on the first day, so a draw seemed an almost inevitable result.

England's start on the Monday, in reply to New Zealand's 249, was not encouraging. The wickets of Charles Barnett, Hutton and Washbrook all fell for 36 runs before Hardstaff went out to join Denis, who was batting at number 4. The great Walter Hammond for some reason was down to bat at number 6. As it happened, his talent was not required to rescue the innings. Hardstaff and Compton put a different complexion on matters by making 125 for the fourth wicket in less than two hours on a slow pitch.

The stand was broken, after Denis had made 65, in just about the unluckiest possible fashion. Hardstaff drove Giff Vivian, a slow left-arm bowler, straight back down the wicket. Vivian stuck out a hand, deflected the ball on to the stumps and Denis, backing up out of his crease, was run out. It was a cruel end to a good innings but an auspicious beginning to a Test career.

Wisden recorded that 'except for a chance when 46 to short leg ... Compton batted extremely well on his debut in Test cricket. There was no mistaking his sound judgement of the ball that could be hit with safety. *Both he and Hardstaff ran splendidly between the wickets.*' (My italics.)

After Hardstaff had scored 103, his second hundred of the series, Walter Robins declared England's first innings closed at 254 for seven. New Zealand then made 187 and England 31 for one. Given a bowl late in New Zealand's innings, Denis responded by taking two wickets for 34 in what must have been six quite eventful overs.

He went back to the Middlesex camp to get 81 against Somerset and, a week later, 111 against Nottinghamshire at Trent Bridge. Hendren also got a hundred; so did the wicket keeper, Jack Price. When Middlesex declared at 525 for nine with a first innings lead of more than 200 it seemed they were on their way towards a crucial victory in the championship. But they were foiled by Joe Hardstaff in a magnificent innings of 243. On either side of the war Joe was a batsman of the highest calibre.

It was entirely fitting that Patsy, in his last championship game against Surrey at Lord's, should bow out with 103 in the first innings. I have to record however that in the second innings he got 103 less. The ovation given to him was as affectionate and as heart-warming as the one that Denis himself was to receive twenty years later.

Denis concluded his season in this game by making 28 and 64, and then reported to Highbury for pleasures on different fields. But Middlesex had one further game to play: a challenge match against Yorkshire over four days at The Oval. Walter Robins considered that his side was at least as good as that of the champions, and wanted to put his theory to the test. There was a good deal of opposition to this challenge but in the end Surrey agreed to lend their ground and Yorkshire agreed to participate provided that no precedent was being set. As it happened, Middlesex got the worst of the weather and pitch, and succumbed by an innings and 115 runs. Even the presence of Denis would have been unlikely to alter the result.

This was the last season not just for Hendren but for Maurice Tate, Andy Sandham and J.C. (Jack) White. Their younger successors in the England side now took a winter's rest from touring and were no doubt none the worse for that. For Len Hutton and Denis Compton the future must have looked rosy indeed. They had clearly established themselves at the highest level and could look forward to many fruitful, unbroken years of success.

1938: Against Bradman and O'Reilly

BY SCORING almost 750 runs in May, Denis started his third season of first-class cricket more than well enough. Yet the spotlight early in 1938 was directed at Don Bradman and Bill Edrich, both of whom completed their 1,000 runs before the end of the month. The Australian captain, repeating a feat he had achieved in England in 1930, got there first, on May 27, when he made a hundred against Hampshire at Southampton.

It so happened that Edrich, who opened for his county in those days, was still short of the target when the Australians came to Lord's for their next match, against Middlesex, and he still needed 10 more after being bowled by Bill O'Reilly for 9 in his first innings. Then, on the last day (May 31) of a game condemned by bad weather to a draw, Bradman generously declared just to give Edrich (who finished with 20 not out) an opportunity that was gratefully accepted. All of Edrich's 1,010 runs were made at Lord's.

Denis had begun the season with two matches for MCC and had made 77 against Yorkshire and exactly 100, in two hours, in his second innings against Surrey. Two matches later, Denis made 163 against Gloucestershire and enjoyed a stand of 304 with Edrich for the second wicket. This was after his old chum from Lord's, Andy Wilson, now the Gloucestershire wicket keeper, had made 130 going in at number 9. The little left-hander, no mean batsman and a most delightful character, recalls with some pleasure how from some way outside the off stump he 'lapped' a ball from Robins that disappeared into the grandstand square on the leg side. 'I saw Denis wink at me from slip, then put his thumbs up. He was genuinely pleased that an old colleague was having a bit of luck.'

Denis was again a member of an MCC side when the Australians made their first visit of the season to Lord's during which Bradman made a flawless 278 in six hours. In Denis's first tussle with Bill O'Reilly, the 'Tiger' took the honours by having Denis lbw for 23. But Denis, 12 not out in the second innings, was in long enough to get a useful sight of a great bowler's style.

In his next match Denis got 134 and 60 against Lancashire, the hundred being the first of seven he was to take off that county's bowling during his career (he made the same number off those of Sussex). These scores were followed by some low ones including 14 made for England against the Rest in a Test trial played in relentlessly chilly weather.

The Australians came to the first Test, at Trent Bridge, unbeaten and having made some massive scores against the counties and Oxbridge during May. When the weather and pitches changed in June the tourists' successful march continued. While there could be no question about the strength of their batting the bowling without Clarrie Grimmett seemed to depend a great deal on the peerless O'Reilly. McCormick, their fastest man, who had been no-balled thirty-five times at Worcester, only rarely lived up to expectations. But they did have 'Chuck' Fleetwood-Smith, a talented unorthodox left armer with considerable powers of spin who despite being savagely treated by Hammond in 1932/33 remained a threat to the England batsmen. Hammond, who had turned amateur before the 1938 season began, was appointed as the new England captain. Denis, less than a month past his 20th birthday, was to make a hundred in his first Test innings against the old enemy, as did Len Hutton, Charlie Barnett and Eddie Paynter. What was more, Barnett got 98 before lunch on the first day, and for good measure Paynter made it a double ton. England's 658 for eight declared remains the only occasion in the history of the series that four batsmen (Hutton 100, Barnett 126, Paynter 216 not out and Compton 102) have made hundreds in one innings.

In spite of the impetus provided by Barnett, England were in a defensive mood, four wickets down, when Denis joined Paynter. These two transformed the situation with a sparkling partnership of 206 in two hours and twenty minutes. Bob Wyatt, former England captain, after witnessing Denis's fine 102, wrote in the *Daily Mail* that here, undoubtedly, was a youngster with a touch of genius. Denis received one generous slice of luck, Bradman at slip to O'Reilly putting him down before he had scored. (Two evenings earlier, on the eve of the match, O'Reilly had invited Denis to his hotel room for a chat; a nice gesture from an old hand to a relative newcomer.) After congratulating Denis at the end of his innings, England's captain offered him some advice. Hammond told him that it was always a good idea against Australia not just to make a hundred but to take fresh guard and settle in for another.

England had the satisfaction of getting rid of Bradman for a mere 51 and of enforcing the follow-on when Australia were bowled out for 411, in which Stan McCabe played one of the truly great Test match innings. In rather less than four hours, and for the most part with tailenders to keep him company, he hit a dazzling 232. Bradman adjured his side to watch from their balcony and told them they might never see its like again. He also said that he wished he could have batted like that himself.

Bill Brown and Bradman made hundreds in the Australians' second innings of 427 for six declared, and the match was drawn.

Denis had time before the second Test match to play a splendid innings of a different character. The Essex leg-spinner, Peter Smith, looked to be bowling Essex to an exciting victory over Middlesex at Chelmsford. Denis won the day by holding his side's batting together on a turning pitch, scoring 87 not out. He needed to make 23 of the 24 runs put on for the tenth wicket with A.D. Baxter, a fast bowler whose batting form was such that his captain, Walter Robins, could not bear to watch a single ball.

The second Test match, a fine game, again drawn, was chiefly memorable for a regal 240 by Hammond which was certainly one of, if not *the* finest Test innings he ever played. Those who saw it still purr with the recollection of the grandeur of his offside strokeplay. Denis got 6, trapped lbw by O'Reilly, but 99 from Paynter and 83 from Les Ames helped England to a total of 494. To this Australia replied with 422, Brown carrying his bat for 206, but after this runs had to be earned the hard way.

England were 76 for five in their second innings when Denis went in at number 7 to join Paynter. McCormick was whistling it past the batsmen's ears and O'Reilly was in his element on an unpleasant pitch. Denis responded by making 76 not out with the air of a masterly veteran.

In his book, *Lord's*, Sir Pelham Warner wrote of Denis: 'He received almost as great a reception as Hammond on the first day, and he deserved it, for at a time of stress and strain he had batted with the judgement, skill and nerve of one who had played in a score of Test matches.' Don Bradman shook him by the hand, observing that it had been one of the best innings he had seen. Eight years earlier, Denis as a youngster aged 12, after sleeping on a camp bed outside Lord's, had watched the Don make a magnificent 254. Because of Denis's effort, Hammond was able to declare England's second innings closed at 242

39

for eight, whereafter Bradman made 102 not out in a total of 204 for six. Another draw.

As it happened, the 76 not out Denis got in this Test match at the end of June was to remain his highest score for the rest of the season – apart from one big and dramatic hundred against Essex. There was a lot of rain about and batsmen generally found it hard going on the uncovered pitches.

At Old Trafford, the third Test match in the series was abandoned because of rain without a ball being bowled.

Denis had to contend with a drying pitch when making a good 45 in the second innings of the Gentlemen–Players match, an encounter which is still remembered, by those of us old enough, for a thrilling hundred by the Sussex left-hander Hugh Bartlett. Flogging the Players' bowling to all parts, he struck 175 not out, including four sixes and twenty-four fours, out of 256 in two hours and three-quarters.

Another left-hander, the peerless Frank Woolley of Kent, who was then in his last season, was honoured with the captaincy of the Players and made second top score of 41 in his first innings when Ken Farnes, bowling exceedingly fast, took eight for 43. The Gentlemen were led by Walter Hammond, who had, uniquely, previously led the Players.

There were further problems for England when Middlesex inflicted on Yorkshire their first defeat of the season. Len Hutton sustained a broken finger on a Lord's 'flier', the injury putting him out of the fourth Test at Headingley. Les Ames was also out of action, so the England selectors called up Fred Price as a last-minute substitute for Paul Gibb, and they asked Bill Edrich to go in first with Charles Barnett.

For all the runs he made for Middlesex, Edrich, with three failures behind him, was badly in need of something substantial at this level – and a change of luck, too. At Trent Bridge he had played on off his boot. At Lord's he had to contend with the fiery McCormick. He was now to receive a perfect googly from O'Reilly and although he made a very useful 28 on a wearing pitch in the second innings, he was not chosen for the final Test.

O'Reilly took ten wickets for 122 runs in the Headingley Test which Australia won by five wickets on the third day.

Bowlers called the tune throughout, and Fleetwood-Smith, with seven wickets, helped O'Reilly to exert a crucial influence. Hammond made the top score, 76, in England's first innings of 223 as did Bradman, 103, in Australia's 242. The Australian spinners then had England out again for 123 and, thanks to a resilient 33 from Lindsay Hassett in murky light, Australia won after experiencing some nasty moments against Doug Wright at his very best.

Their victory in a tense, low-scoring match ensured, at worst, a share of the rubber and therefore the certain retention of the Ashes which had been won back in England in 1934 and subsequently kept by Australia in 1936/37 when they won a remarkable series after going two down against Gubby Allen's side.

In his first innings Denis was comprehensively bowled by O'Reilly for 14. In his second he had the ill luck to be caught behind off the back of his glove from an unplayable O'Reilly delivery which reared up and gave him no chance. With Denis out, it was bad news for England with only Price, Verity, Wright, Farnes and Bowes occupying the remaining places in the batting order.

Denis now had six matches to play for Middlesex before the final Test. In the first five he made some useful scores. It was only in the last game that he returned to his radiant best when he made his fifth hundred of the summer, 180 not out, against Essex at Lord's, in a mere two and a half hours. This was just the prescription to put him in a good frame of mind for the Oval Test match which followed.

The final Test was, as Ian Peebles has suggested, more a collector's piece than a good match, and imprinted in cricket history as the one in which Len Hutton made a record 364 in a record England total of 903 for seven wickets declared. Len also of course had been a young man when Don Bradman first came to England in 1930. He was 14 when he watched him score 309 in one day during the Headingley Test, and 334 altogether. Now, aged 22, he batted for thirteen hours and seventeen minutes to make 364, a new Test record which not only surpassed Bradman's record in the England–Australia Test series but the 336 not out made by Walter Hammond against New Zealand in 1932/33.

There is a well-known story that towards the end of a partnership between Hutton and Maurice Leyland which realised 382 for the second wicket, Eddie Paynter bet Denis a pound against the pair of them making more than 10 runs altogether. It may have been Denis who laid the bet. Paynter was lbw to O'Reilly for 0 and Denis was bowled by Mervyn Waite for a single. Denis's wicket was the only one the medium paced Waite acquired in the series and in his Test career – a fact which he never failed to remind Denis about whenever they bumped into each other again. Waite has always stood the drinks.

I should add that England won the toss for the fourth time in a row, Maurice Leyland making 187 and Joe Hardstaff 169 not out.

Another familiar story about the innings concerns Arthur Wood, who kept wicket for England in the absence of Les Ames, who was injured. Wood returned to the dressing room after making 53, the score then standing on 876 for seven. 'Just like me,' he said, 'getting out in a bluddy crisis.'

The 900 was about to be posted when Bradman, bowling his third over of leg-breaks, suffered a minor fracture of his right ankle as he caught his boot in a foothold. Having assured himself that the Australian captain could take no further part, Hammond then declared the innings closed after a few more runs were scored. Bradman was never paid a greater compliment.

Australia, without Bradman and their opening batsman, Jack Fingleton, who was also unable to bat, were bowled out for 201 and 123. England won in four days by a margin – an innings and 579 runs – which looks for ever safe in the record books. The series was thus squared at one all, and for once in a way Bradman found himself upstaged in the Test batting averages. He averaged 108, against Hutton's 118. In all first-class games, however, he found himself on a familiar pedestal with 2,429 runs at an average of 115.

Although taking a modest seventh place in England's Test batting (42.80) Denis had made a certain mark with two outstanding innings. In all his first-class matches he made 1,868 runs at 45.56, 1,195 of them in the county championship at just under 50. Edrich, with six hundreds in all his games and 2,378 first-class runs, comfortably headed his county's averages at 64.42. But Middlesex had to settle again for second place behind Yorkshire in the county championship.

When the season was finished, Denis attended Hendon Magistrates Court to explain how it came about that he had been caught for speeding on his way to the second Test Match. The chairman observed that it had been a memorable Test match in many ways, and the fine would be forty shillings.

Denis was asked if he would be available to tour South Africa with the MCC team in the following winter, but at that time Arsenal had a prior claim on his services.

The 1939 *Wisden* named him as one of their five cricketers of the year, having bestowed the same distinction on Len Hutton in the previous issue. 'An adaptable player with a touch of genius, Compton possesses a sound defence, a wonderful eye and the right stroke for every ball.

He is particularly strong on the leg side and his confidence, coolness and resource are remarkable for so young a player.'

1939: His Finest Summer So Far

IN THE LAST season of first-class cricket before the United Kingdom went to war, Denis enjoyed his most successful summer to date. He scored 2,468 runs, almost 500 more than his previous best, and he averaged more than 50 (56.09) for the first time. Three years' experience had mellowed his judgement without in any way inducing a change of style or approach.

The first of his eight hundreds that season was a big one, 181 against Essex at Lord's. Laurie Gray, the Middlesex number 11, went out to join him just after he had reached three figures, whereupon Denis thrashed another brilliant 78 runs in an hour while his partner made just a single. He then had his first taste of West Indian fast bowling and found it to his liking on an amiable pitch as he got 115 for MCC against Rolph Grant's touring side.

This was West Indies' third tour of England, where they had yet to win a Test match, but they had savoured success on their own wickets in 1934/35 when winning a four-match series 2–1 against an MCC team whose batting included R.E.S. Wyatt (captain), Walter Hammond, Maurice Leyland, Patsy Hendren and Leslie Ames.

In 1939 Learie Constantine and Manny Martindale were again the spearhead of the West Indian attack, and George Headley was there once more to carry their batting. Headley was to finish his tour with 1,745 runs at an average of 72, more than 40 better than any of his colleagues could manage. Constantine, with 103 victims, took his 100 wickets as he had done in 1928. If the pace of Martindale and Constantine was not quite as fearsome as it had been, the charismatic Learie still provided a remarkable, sometimes eccentric, variety of all sorts of bowling.

Denis's hundreds against Essex and West Indies were followed by consistent high scoring at Lord's during the second half of May. He made 94 against Northants, 44 and 46 against Gloucestershire, 143 against Hampshire and 81 and 50 not out against Sussex before the West Indians came back to thrash Middlesex by an innings and 228 runs. Headley scored 227, Derek Sealy 181 and Jeffrey Stollmeyer, then only 19 years of age, 117 in a West Indian total of 665. Denis's three wickets for 67 made for much better reading than those who had nought – or little better – for plenty. But he made only 13 and 26 as Middlesex were outplayed. At Frome, where Harold Gimblett in 1935 had marked his first-class debut with a hundred in sixty-three minutes, Denis now won the game against Somerset with a masterful 103 not out on a worn pitch in the second innings. But in his next match, when Yorkshire came to Lord's, Middlesex found themselves on the wrong end of the stick. Herbert Sutcliffe in his last season for Yorkshire got 175 and Maurice Leyland 180 not out on a benign pitch. Middlesex did not help their own cause by dropping both batsmen early in their innings. Then, when they batted, they found themselves trapped by Hedley Verity on a drying surface. Denis did well to make 25 and 18 as Middlesex went down to another massive innings defeat.

Denis was soon back on song with 47 and 111 not out at Northampton, the second innings taking him eighty-two minutes as he and Jack Robertson, who made his maiden first-class century, hurried Middlesex to an easy win. He then made 120 in his first Test against the West Indies, just as he had done against Australia a year before.

This one was especially notable in that during its course Denis had a relatively rare but memorable partnership with Len Hutton who made 196 and thus achieved the same double. They added 248 for the fourth wicket in only two hours and twenty minutes, Hutton responding to Denis's carefree approach by unfurling those glorious strokes which he could always offer when the mood took him. Denis was put down twice early on – two difficult chances off Martindale – so his exciting innings was not flawless. Hutton got his last 96 runs in even time.

Another noteworthy feature of the game was provided by Headley, who scored two hundreds, just as he had done against England in a Caribbean Test match in 1929/30. He was a great cutter and hooker who liked to get on the back foot. As with all the greatest players, he seemed to see the ball just a fraction earlier than lesser batsmen, and to play it later. Despite Headley's effort the Hutton–Compton stand ensured that their side took a big first innings lead of 127 runs. West Indies, bowled out again for 225, were beaten by eight wickets on the third and final day. Bill Copson, the sandy-haired Derbyshire fast bowler, had nine wickets in the match.

Back with Middlesex again, Denis got 115 in Bill Farrimond's benefit match at Old Trafford, his third hundred in consecutive matches. In this one, according to *Wisden*, he enjoyed some luck in the way of chances spilled. He had a good game for the Players against the Gentlemen, 58 and 70, got 40 for Arthur Wood's benefit at Park Avenue, Bradford and, next, played a staggeringly good innings of 80, while all about him struggled, on a quixotic pitch made to measure for seam bowlers at Derby. Ian Peebles has told how Denis ran him out when asking him to embark on an unlikely second run to third man. The fielder hit the stumps direct. In the next over Denis suffered exactly the same fate.

The following Middlesex fixture, against Nottinghamshire, was an oddity in that they played it at The Oval, Lord's being required on the Saturday for the Eton and Harrow game. Denis got 65 in his second innings.

Manchester's weather in 1939 did not deal their Test match so shabby a hand as it had done a year earlier. Rain nevertheless permitted barely more than half an hour's play on the first day and put back the start of proceedings on the second. Inevitably the match was drawn, with England declaring twice (at 164 for seven and 128 for six) but lacking time to force another victory. West Indies made 133, with Bill Bowes of Yorkshire celebrating his 31st birthday by taking six for 33 and four for 43.

England's first innings included a lovely 76 from Joe Hardstaff. Denis's efforts were modest despite his earlier form. He got 4 before he trod on his stumps when aiming to hook the leg-spinner Bertie Clarke. As I have remarked, he tended to make such full use of the crease that his occasional dismissal in this fashion could be no real surprise. In the second innings he made a solid 34 not out.

Denis now returned to Lord's for another crack at Derbyshire's bowlers, and crack is perhaps the best word to use. On this occasion he hit 214 not out, his first double hundred, and in the process passed 2,000 runs for the season. If it is a moot point whether he was an even better player of leg spin than off spin, there can be no doubt that he now relished his only confrontation with Tommy Mitchell, an England bowler, as much as he had done with Tich Freeman in his first season. Mitchell's bowling could on occasion be touched by something approaching genius. On this day, though, he conceded 95 in seventeen overs.

The end of Denis's season was undistinguished, although he halted a brief run of low scores by making 52 and 68 for Middlesex against Surrey at The Oval. One of those low scores had come in the previous game, at Canterbury, when 'Big Jim' Smith flayed Kent's bowling to the tune of seven sixes and five fours in an innings of 101 not out in eighty-one minutes. It was his first and only hundred. As the sixes disappeared over the marquees and the lime tree in a predictable arc between long-on and square-leg, the captain Ian Peebles held up the other end while Jim made 98 out of their stand of 116 for the last wicket.

The third and final Test, at The Oval, was a high-scoring affair, played on one of the blandest wickets prepared by the long-serving 'Bosser' Martin. Although a draw was inevitable, there were some fireworks from the West Indian batsmen which have lingered in the memory. After England had made 352, with Hardstaff contributing a polished innings of 94, the left-handed Kenneth Weekes, who was known as 'Bam Bam', made an extremely brisk 137 and Constantine an out-rageous 79 in a West Indies total of 498. Weekes, who was a cousin of the better known Everton, struck his runs in two and a quarter hours.

Constantine went even faster as he flogged the bowling of Maurice Nichols and Reg Perks to all parts of The Oval, the England field then being dispersed by Hammond as it would be nowadays in the latter overs of a one-day fixture in an effort to stem the tide on a Sunday afternoon. One astounding shot by Constantine, off the back foot against Perks, soared for six to the Vauxhall end, a prodigious carry which I can still see now, fifty years later. R.C. Robertson-Glasgow was moved to reflect whether in the whole history of Test matches England bowling had been so lashed and banged and rattled.

The stumps were drawn when Hammond declared England's second innings closed at 366 for three. Hutton, who made 165 not out, had scored well over 1,000 runs in his last eight Test matches. Denis, who had got 21 in his first innings, was 10 not out.

Nine days later Denis strapped on his pads for Middlesex for the last time that season and went out to make 86 against Warwickshire at Lord's while Jack Robertson and Bill Edrich also got hundreds. The storm clouds of war now rumbled ever closer. West Indies went home to the Caribbean, their last seven fixtures unfulfilled, and MCC's tour of India, in 1939/40, was cancelled. Denis would not bat again for his county side for seven years.

For the fourth consecutive summer, and for a third behind Yorkshire, Middlesex had to settle for second place in the championship. Denis topped his county's batting averages for the first time with 1,853 runs, including six hundreds, at an average of 61.76. Bill Edrich came next with 1,948 (from four more innings) and seven hundreds at 52.64. Jack Robertson, maintaining his promise of 1938, was third. This was the first season that the Middlesex batting order began with Robertson and Sidney Brown followed by Edrich at number three and Denis at four.

In all matches Edrich got more than 2,000 runs for a third year running but he did not play for England this year, in spite of making 219 in the final, timeless Test at Durban on the MCC tour of South Africa in 1938/39. That innings followed Test scores of 4,10,0,6 and 1 in that series – and those came after he had made, 5, 0, 10, 12, 28 and 12 against Australia in 1938. He was not to represent his country again until MCC went to Australia in 1946/47. Walter Hammond headed the first-class batting averages for the seventh successive season, a record he was to make yet more remarkable when cricket was resumed in 1946. But it seemed significant that in 1939 L. Hutton stood second in the list and D. Compton third.

The War Years

WHEN ENGLAND DECLARED WAR on Germany in September 1939 Denis sought straight away to serve his country. After a couple of months with the reserve police force he was enrolled, at the end of December, in the 90th A.A. Field Regiment Royal Artillery at East Grinstead in Sussex. One of his initial responsibilities was to maintain and stoke up the station's coal fires, which must have been an agreeable task in one of the worst winters in memory.

Happily enough, it was soon recognized by the authorities that the services of well-known sportsmen might be more gainfully employed. By the early spring of 1940 Denis had been posted to Aldershot on a course which soon revealed that the standards of fitness required of physical training instructors in the Army were very different to those of a professional cricketer. I imagine to-day's players would find the transition rather less arduous. Suffice to say that although Denis began a new regime with the advantages of natural athleticism and the harsher experiences of a professional footballer, the Army made him fitter than he had been at any other time before or since. He lost a stone in weight, which had a positive effect on his soccer activities.

He had not been long at Aldershot when he found himself under the command of Col R. S. Rait-Kerr, who had become secretary of MCC in 1936 but had now temporarily resumed his military career. It is thought that the Colonel never quite saw Denis as having the orderly and disciplined attitude necessary to make a natural soldier, but he was flexible enough to allow an outstanding cricketer and footballer ample opportunities to entertain a public then starved of sporting entertainment. In March 1940 Denis went to Paris to play football for the British Army against their French counterparts. Several months later he represented the Army against the RAF in a match at Lord's which was interrupted, but not abandoned, due to aerial action in the Battle of Britain.

I leave his major football exploits in war-time to the next chapter. In cricketing fixtures of no great moment or pressure, his experiences were largely unspectacular. Come the winter of 1943/44, however, he was to be given a chance to deploy his batting skills in a very different climate. In January 1944, having just scored a hat-trick of goals for Arsenal against Luton Town, Company Sergeant Major Compton took the night train from Euston to Liverpool and set sail for India, where he was to remain until after the Japanese had surrendered in 1945. Denis subsequently was made captain of a Services' football team which included Ted Ditchburn, the Tottenham Hotspur goalkeeper, and travelled, unbeaten in fifty matches, the length and breadth of Burma to bring joy to Services' outposts where something unusual was required to mitigate a sense of ennui and anticlimax. The debilitating humidity enabled Denis to shed some of the weight he had put on again during two good seasons of Indian cricket.

Finding the hard, true pitches in India very much to his liking, he played seventeen first-class innings in 1944/45 and 1945/46, averaging almost 90. One of his games, against the Parsees in the Bombay Pentangular Tournament at the Brabourne stadium, was for a European XI which included some notable names: Joe Hardstaff, Reg Simpson, Dick Howorth (Worcestershire), Peter Cranmer (Warwickshire), Paddy Corrall (Leicestershire wicket keeper) and Peter Judge (Glamorgan). Denis made 76 not out in his second innings; Hardstaff got 159 and 79. In another match, when he scored a hundred for a Services XI against the Cricket Club of India, he had his first good look at Vijay Merchant who got an unbeaten double century in a total of 615 for four declared. Runs on those pitches were not difficult to come by. If it was too hot for Denis to sally down the pitch, he stayed in his ground and took his pleasures off the back foot.

But of all the games Denis played in India the one best chronicled is that between Holkar and Bombay in the final for the Ranji Trophy. Holkar, in the most intense heat, were set to make a huge total in the last innings but Denis and Mushtaq Ali had a substantial partnership. Even after the tall and dashing Indian left-hander had been dismissed, Denis continued to sweat it out – for an eminently sound reason.

A rich businessman of Holkar had promised him 50 rupees for every run he scored in excess of 100. So on and on he went, feeling more affluent for every weary stroke until, after a record Indian last wicket stand, he carried out his bat for 249 not out, then the highest score of his career. The balance in his favour was calculated at around 7,500 rupees – about £600 in English currency at the time. But, alas, the rich merchant, so Denis was informed, had been called away on an urgent visit to Calcutta. Denis never saw him again.

A story, rather less well known, concerns a game in which Denis played alongside Keith Miller. They had first met each other in an inter-Services game in England in 1943, before Miller had taken up bowling seriously. 'Comp was a young hero to me then, with his pre-war record,' Keith recalls. 'I idolised the guy. He was run out by yards in the first game we played together, and the same thing happened on our way home through India, but he got a hundred in his second innings.' Keith by then was returning to Australia with their Services team. He came up against Denis again in their match with East Zone, in Calcutta, which was played at a time of student unrest.

The students' leader had in fact been their host at a reception on the evening before a riot started. Denis was going strongly in the middle when the situation took a distinctly nasty turn. Cristofani, the Australian leg-spinner, checked his approach as this student rushed up to Denis and said, 'Mr Compton, you very good cricketer, but you must go.' So he did. Keith Miller says that for ever afterwards when he was fielding and Denis came out to bat, he greeted him with the same words. All this helped to forge a long-enduring friendship between two charismatic players whose reputations and approaches to the game had so much in common.

In the same Indian season Denis made 91 and 114 for the Europeans against the Hindus in Bombay. Charles Palmer, then of Worcestershire but later of Leicestershire and England – and chairman of the TCCB – says that Denis not only ran him out with the greatest of ease but did the same to one or two others as well.

There is just one further tale to relate about Denis's war-time days in India, and he tells it himself with some relish. It appears that at some time or other a young soldier, name of Zia, was given guidance by Denis at the nets. Many years later, when Pakistan were due to play an important Test against India, President Zia sent a telex to London saying that he must have Denis Compton to stay with him for the big match. Lord Carrington, then Foreign Secretary, is said to have been greatly impressed.

Reverting to his earlier life on a less lofty plane, Denis came home to collect his demob suit at Olympia towards the end of 1945, and to link up once more with his brother Leslie, whose platoon in the Middlesex Regiment had been the first to enter Belsen.

Denis as Footballer

WHEN DENIS SIGNED amateur forms for Arsenal and joined the staff at Highbury in 1932 he was encouraged to play for Hampstead Town which was then the top amateur club in his vicinity. But it was Nunhead, in the Isthmian League, which soon became a nursery for Arsenal's promising youngsters and the one which fostered Denis's game. At school he had been a left half. Now he was cast as a left winger. As Cliff Bastin was the Arsenal and England left winger, and at that time the rest of the club's forward line read (left to right) Alex James, Jack Lambert, David Jack and Joe Hulme (who was a Middlesex cricketer), he wondered how long it might take him to earn a place in the most glamorous side in the land. Herbie ('Stopper') Roberts held sway at centre half, with George Male and Eddie Hapgood at full-back, and Frank Moss in goal. James and Bastin remained up front when Ted Drake took over as centre forward in 1934. Arsenal won the League Championship five times in the 30s.

The famous Arsenal manager, Herbert Chapman, had died when his successor, George Allison, signed Denis as a professional footballer on his 17th birthday, in 1935. After some games for the Arsenal 'A' team as well as for their Reserves side he made his first team debut in a friendly fixture against Glasgow Rangers at Highbury in the early days of the 1936/37 season.

This was followed soon afterwards by his first appearance in the League, a 2–2 draw with Derby County. He had the thrill of scoring his side's first goal. Then he got another, in a 2–0 win over Charlton Athletic at The Valley. Alex James in his long baggy pants laid it on for him with a beautifully judged long through pass. 'Keep out on the wing, lad,' the little man said, 'and I'll know where you are.' It was to be the start of a long relationship of mutual respect and affection.

Denis held on to his first team place until an indifferent game against Everton on Boxing Day saw him dropped back to the Reserves. When the war came he had made 22 appearances for the 1st XI. His brother Leslie had made 59. Leslie, who had preceded him on the Highbury staff, was moved from left full-back to centre half but remained overshadowed in the pre-war years first by Herbie Roberts and then by Bernard Joy. The two England caps Leslie won in 1950/51, when Denis was cricketing in Australia, came as belated recognition for his under-rated talents.

One further (pre-war) incident in Denis's story needs to be mentioned. At The Valley in 1938 he was involved in a collision with the Charlton player, Sid Hobbins, which resulted in the removal of a cartilage from his right knee. It was to be the best part of a decade before the knee played him up again. After Denis had suffered the belated effects of the injury for some time, Sid Hobbins had the thought and kindness to write him a letter in which he said, 'I am terribly sorry for the trouble I have caused you over all these years.'

Wartime football had to be organized on a regional basis. Arsenal shared the White Hart Lane pitch with Tottenham Hotspur, and the Compton brothers, still stationed in England, were able to play a regular part. Leslie was moved again, this time to emergency centre forward. On one occasion he scored ten goals, six of them with his head, as Arsenal demolished Clapton Orient 15–2. This explains how in the wartime Leagues Leslie comfortably stood at the head of the Arsenal goal-scoring list with 29.

In the first leg of the League South Cup Final against Preston North End at Wembley in 1940/41, Denis, on the left wing, scored the goal which helped Arsenal draw 1–1. Unfortunately Arsenal lost the second leg 1–2. In the League South Cup Final of 1942/43 he scored one of Arsenal's seven goals against Charlton, Leslie having returned to full-back. They then met Blackpool, League North Cup winners, but went down 2–4 at Stamford Bridge.

By 1943 Denis was an established wartime international, having made his England debut against Wales at Wembley in April 1940, a match which Wales won by a single goal. Five months earlier his brother had been selected to play against Wales in Cardiff. In all but the first of his eleven wartime or Victory internationals Denis was never in a losing England side.

In April 1943, when Leslie was at full-back, Denis got a first goal for his country when England beat Scotland 4–0 in front of 105,000 spectators at Hampden Park. Not long afterwards the two brothers were in the same England side for the last time, in a 1–1 draw with Wales in Cardiff. Denis completed his wartime internationals in a blaze of English glory.

In September 1943 he got another goal as Wales were beaten 8–3 at Wembley. Three weeks later he was a member of the side which thrashed Scotland 8–0 at Maine Road, Manchester. Tommy Lawton got four of them, including a hat-trick in the space of ten minutes. In Jack Rollin's *Soccer at War* Frank Swift is quoted as saying that this was the finest team he ever played in, so I am sure that it is worth setting out in detail. It read: Swift (Manchester City); Laurie Scott (Arsenal), George Hardwick (Middlesbrough); Cliff Britton (Everton), Stan Cullis (Wolverhampton Wanderers) (captain), Joe Mercer (Everton); Stanley Matthews (Stoke City), Raich Carter (Sunderland), Tommy Lawton (Everton), Jimmy Hagan (Sheffield United) and Denis Compton (Arsenal). Within three months of the match, Denis was on his way to India.

Soon after his return home and demobilisation in 1946 he played his last game for England in the Victory international against Scotland at Hampden Park, watched by a vast crowd of 139,468 spectators. England lost it by a single goal scored by Jimmy Delaney (Manchester United). Swift, Scott, Hardwick, Mercer, Lawton and Hagan still wore England's colours. Billy Wright (Wolves), Neil Franklin (Stoke), Billy Elliott (West Bromwich Albion) and Len Shackleton (Bradford Park Avenue) were Denis's latest colleagues.

In this match Denis, now carrying more weight than before, implored his half-back, Joe Mercer, to play it close. There was a moment, however, when Joe forgot his brief. A long ball was exactly angled to the corner, and Denis set off in desperate pursuit. He caught up with it but his momentum was such that he took ball and flag-post out of play with him, and finished up making a dramatic belly landing.

In his last three footballing seasons, before he retired from the game after the Cup Final of 1950, he was never again quite the force he had been in the early years of war. The knee must have had a lot to do with that and almost certainly, in the light of all the bother and pain it gave him, he played one season too many. But he and Leslie had the pleasure of gaining League Winners' medals with Arsenal in 1947/48 – a unique distinction in that they had both also played for the champion cricket county in the previous summer. They also played together in Arsenal's victory over Liverpool in the FA Cup Final at Wembley at the end of the 1949/50 season.

Denis took part in that match, as he had done all season, with his knee heavily strapped. At half time, things not having gone at all well for him, his manager, Tom Whittaker, said, 'You've got forty-five minutes left, so go out there and give it all you've got.' What is more, he fortified his left winger with a stiff brandy which worked wonders.

A great competitor left the game on a suitable note and Arsenal, captained by Joe Mercer, won 2–0.

No one has any doubt about Denis's stature as a cricketer, but just how good a footballer was he? Geoffrey Green, erstwhile distinguished football correspondent of *The Times*, holds that he was a useful club winger but not really of international calibre. 'His strength was a natural left foot. He centred well and quite often got a useful goal. He *played* at cricket but *worked* at football.'

Peter Williams, a staunch Arsenal supporter on either side of the war, whose opinion I respect, takes much the same line. 'Left-footed, yes. And one-footed, yes. The regular supporters didn't rate him that highly. His 'bad leg' was a big handicap after the war, of course, but statistics show that he only played 49 games for his club in the League, and five in the Cup. His big rival for the left wing position post-war was Ian McPherson, a great player who appeared more than three times as often.'

Such views are echoed by Doug Insole, an England Test cricketer who often watched Denis playing for Arsenal with the knowledgeable eye of one who had gained a football Blue at Cambridge. 'He had a tremendous left foot, but no right. And another odd thing, in total contrast with his cricket: he could be a very petulant and niggly soccer player. Les used to look after him.' Another Essex and England cricketer, and Cambridge soccer Blue, is Trevor Bailey, who has written about football for many years. 'Denis had a lovely feel for the game,' he says. 'He seemed always to be in the right place at the right time.'

Denis's greatest playing contemporaries on the football scene whose opinions I have sought are united in praise, none more so than Joe Mercer. 'In the early war years he was quite magnificent. He was some player then, something a bit special, very brave with a great left foot and he scored some cracking goals. He was the best left wing I ever played behind. And he was so modest; we all loved him.' The incomparable Sir Stanley Matthews rates him as an outstanding winger: 'He was a strong player with excellent ball control and a deadly left foot. He had the speed, too, and he always gave 100 per cent.'

Stan Cullis, who was often Denis's captain in wartime matches, thinks some soccer reporters were rather unkind. 'I resented this because I was always delighted to have him in my side. He was unorthodox – in many ways a one-off just as he was in cricket. I never met a more charming, likeable bloke or one with such a dazzling sense of humour.' Stan admits that the hair loss he began to suffer at about the age of 19 was accentuated by the addition of Denis to teams under his charge. 'We travelled by train to Newcastle-on-Tyne and, there being no manager in those days, I was booking the players into the Station hotel when Denis told me he'd left his boots in the carriage. We had to organize a search party in the sidings.

'I remember another occasion at Wembley, England *v* Scotland, when I had to get my players out on the pitch in good time for presentation to Field Marshal Montgomery. No sign of Compton. I thought I knew where he was, so I sent a message saying that if he didn't get to the dressing room pronto I'd leave him out of the side. Denis eventually appeared with precious little time to get changed. And what do you think his first words were to our trainer? He says, "Can you put a few studs in my boots?"

'When Denis was stationed at Aldershot early on in the war he used to drive to the station and from there go by rail to London to play for Arsenal. When he arrived home again one night, his wife happened to remark that she hadn't heard the noise of his car. No wonder: he'd left it at the station.'

I saw Denis play several games for Arsenal in the late '40s but, not feeling qualified to make a personal judgement on his footballing skills, remain content to accept the ratings by his peers.

1946: Into the Prime Years

IN 1946 DENIS WAS TO EMBARK on the most exciting period of his cricketing career and, freed at last from the anxieties and horrors of war, England's supporters flocked back to the first-class game with a grateful feeling that at least one old pleasure could be savoured again. County membership figures climbed to record levels which club administrators, in spite of all the problems posed by austere post-war conditions, coped with adequately enough.

When first-class cricket began again in 1919, after the Great War, those players who had not lost their lives in the conflict had missed four years of participation. In 1946, the professionals had seen six seasons pass by. This hiatus was hard on those whose careers were moving towards an end in 1939, while it can only be idle conjecture to wonder just what cricketers in the early stages of their careers like Denis and Len Hutton might have achieved if the world had remained at peace.

Denis was 27 when he buckled on his pads for Middlesex again; Len was approaching his 30th birthday. Yet both could hope that the best might well be yet to come, and there was profound relief for all *aficionados* when Len provided evidence that he had largely overcome the effects of a serious war-time injury. A fracture of his left arm during Commando training had left it shorter and weaker than his right. Only a batsman of supreme skills could have made the necessary adjustments to his technique.

Bill Edrich had just turned 30 when he began again with Middlesex. To have been rated, as a Norfolk farmer, in a reserved occupation during the war had been no more to his liking than to be told, after he had conquered this problem, that he was too old to fly in the Royal Air Force. He got over that one, too. Piloting a Beaufighter he finished his war with a DFC and a record number of sorties.

Denis began his first post-war season on an inauspicious note. For MCC against Surrey, he scored 0 and 20, falling victim to Alf Gover and Alec Bedser respectively. He soon hit his familiar stride, however. In mid-May he made 147 not out and 54 run out against Northants at Lord's. Towards the end of the month he hit two hundreds in a match, 124 and 100, for the first time in his career. These he took off the Lancashire bowlers at Old Trafford, which was always one of his favourite grounds. Then, for no consistently obvious reason, he began a sequence of dispiritingly low scores, interrupted by one big innings at Fenner's.

When Nottinghamshire came to Lord's he made 10, bowled by Arthur Jepson, and 0 not out. The conditions for what play the rain allowed were not easy for batsmen. Then he scored 7 and 1 against Derbyshire on what I believe was the only occasion he went in first for Middlesex except when his side needed runs in the last innings against the clock. He fell twice to the Derbyshire leg-spinner Albert Ennion Growcott Rhodes, who must then, I think, have been bowling 'seam up' on a greenish pitch.

After these three failures, he hit form with a dazzling 202, in even time, for Middlesex against Cambridge University at Fenner's. According to E. W. Swanton, when Denis, his first hundred completed, sent a message to his skipper enquiring what he should do next, he got the reply from Walter Robins, 'Do? What about a few strokes? We haven't seen anything yet.' Ten of the next twelve balls went to various parts of the boundary. After this performance, he hit a slump; his next six innings brought him four noughts and a total of only six runs.

It was only rarely that Denis failed to show the flag in a benefit match – his own or anyone else's. Unfortunately, in the Whitsun game against Sussex, when Jim Sims was the beneficiary, Denis was bowled by James Langridge, slow left arm, for no score. Then came the first of two Test trials, at Lord's, in which Jack Martin of Kent bowled him with a fast inswinging yorker, for 0 again. Next, in Middlesex's home match with Yorkshire, played throughout on a difficult pitch, Frank Smailes had him excitingly caught at short leg by Brian Sellers for 8 in his first innings, and lbw for another 0 in his second. In his last innings before the start of the next Test series, against India, he managed to get off the mark against Glamorgan in Swansea but was promptly bowled by Johnny Clay for a single.

With scores of 0, 0, 8, 0 and 1 immediately behind him, Denis's feelings as he went out to bat in England's first innings at Lord's can be readily imagined. He desperately needed a bit of luck. But, alas, he was bowled first ball by Amarnath, his bat tangling with the front pad on its downswing.

He did not bat again until Warwickshire came to play Middlesex at Lord's four days later. By this stage a time-honoured dressing-room ritual – which sock, which boot, which pad to put on first, sleeves rolled up or down, cap or no cap – was subject to frequent and perhaps desperate changes as he sought to change his luck. He walked out to bat against Eric Hollies wearing a cap – his first England one – which was highly unusual. An inside edge off a jabbed, uncertain stroke spun back to hit his stumps without dislodging a bail. Believing that the fates were on his side, he swung violently against the next ball, more in hope than in anger, and middled it for four. He went on to make 122. Denis has admitted that it was not one of his best innings, but that it was important; he had played himself back into form, and out of the worst run of low scores he had yet experienced in his first-class career. The crisis was over. Although it so happened that he made only 3 in his next innings, against Nottinghamshire at Trent Bridge, the runs came freely again for the rest of his season.

A young Fred Titmus was in the crowd to see Denis turn the tide. He had been a faithful spectator, hoping for better things, during the earlier misadventures. In those days Fred was a very promising inside left who played for Chelsea Youth and Watford Reserves. His idols, including Denis, were those who frequented Highbury's marbled halls. Fred was asked by a friend to go to Lord's to watch Compton. 'I thought Denis was a marvellous footballer,' Fred now says, 'but I asked my friend, "Does he play cricket?" ' I suspect this quote may be taken with a pinch of salt, but there can be no doubting another. 'I first met Compo when I joined the Middlesex staff in 1949. He was a hero to me then, and he still is.'

Let me now return to the first match in the three-Test series against India. The touring side was captained by the Nawab of Pataudi senior, who had played three Test matches for England against Australia in the early thirties. The team included experienced players such as Vijay Merchant, Mushtaq Ali, Amarnath, C. S. Nayudu, Hindlekar and Banerjee, all of whom had toured England in 1936.

They were now joined by younger players, notably Vijay Hazare, R. S. Modi and Mulwantrai Himmatlal (better known as Vinoo) Mankad, who had developed their skills in conditions not greatly affected by the war. But in a wet, cold English summer many in the side were vulnerable. The exceptions were Merchant who scored 2,385 first-class runs at an average of almost 75, and Mankad, who did the double – the first (and last) touring cricketer to achieve the feat since Learie Constantine for the West Indies in 1928.

Although Denis had come out of his batting slump, it was not until the rain affected second Test at Old Trafford that he showed the Indians the best of his skills.

Walter Hammond won the toss at Lord's, whereupon Alec Bedser signalled his arrival on the Test match scene by taking seven wickets for 49 as India were bowled out for 200. England replied with 428, with the elegant Joe Hardstaff making 205, the largest and the last of his Test match hundreds. Bedser then took another four wickets in India's second innings of 275, making it simple for England to win by ten wickets just before lunch on the third and final day.

Back now to Denis and to Middlesex for whom he promptly made his fourth hundred of the summer, 115, and 55 not out against Hampshire. The next century came in the following fixture, a second Test trial at Canterbury. He got 103 in even time against the England XI, the selectors having chosen him to buttress the Rest. A week later he scored a rapid 87 in the Gentlemen–Players match before proceeding to Old Trafford for the second Test.

It rained for most of the week. The match eventually started late with England being asked to bat first on a slow pitch. Hutton, Washbrook and Hammond all got 50s or more. Denis joined them by making 51 out of 75 in seventy-five minutes before Amarnath had him lbw with an inswinger that kept low. England got 294 to which Merchant and Mushtaq Ali replied with 124 for the first wicket. However, all ten Indian wickets fell for another 46 runs, four of them to Bedser and five to the local bowler Dick Pollard of Lancashire.

The 71 not out that Denis got in England's second innings, on a genuine sticky dog, was probably the finest he played all summer. It was fascinating to observe his judgement of what and what not to play against the formidable bowling of Amarnath whose lively pace had the ball rearing off a length and moving off the seam, or of Mankad with spiteful left-arm spin and lift. This innings was an object lesson in the art of batting in such conditions. Since England were at one time 84 for five, and in clear danger of being bowled out, it was just as well that he held the fort so staunchly.

Hammond was able to declare at 153 for five and India, finishing on 152 for nine, just managed to make a draw of it. Bedser shone this time with seven for 52, which gave him a haul of 22 wickets in his first two matches for England at an average of less than 11. It was to be very different in Australia the following winter. But Alec always had his large feet firmly planted on the ground.

In his next two matches for Middlesex Denis toyed with Kent's bowling to make 142 on the Mote ground in Maidstone and did much the same when striking 121 at Hove against Sussex. Then, in the third

Test at The Oval, he made 24 not out in his only innings. The match was reduced by rain to only seven and a half hours of play and thus inevitably drawn.

This was a Test in which Indian batting, that of their opening batsmen at least, did itself something like justice. Merchant made a refined 128 before being run out by Denis in unusual circumstances. He was sent back by Mankad, and Denis, running behind the bowler from mid-on, used his deadly left foot to kick the ball on to the stumps. India got 331, England 95 for three, and that was that. In England's last innings, Hammond had enough time to become the first batsman to pass the 7,000 mark in Test cricket. England won the series by virtue of their success at Lord's.

A few days later Denis made what was then his highest score in England, 235 against Surrey at Lord's. In the later stages of a partnership with Edrich which put on 296 runs in three and three-quarter hours, the Surrey captain, Holmes, decided that he might do worse than call for a new ball. Jim Swanton has written that seven of the next eight balls from Gover and Bedser were dispatched for four with strokes of the finest Compton pedigree.

Just two days after he scored 76 against Essex he was on his way to Australia for the 1946/47 Test series. Middlesex's victory over Essex, the third in their last four games, ensured that they would finish the championship as runners-up once more. Yorkshire, under Brian Sellers, had already made certain of their fourth successive title and twenty-second in all.

In his first-class matches in 1946 Denis scored more hundreds (nine) and more runs (2,403) than anyone else. His average of 61.61 was bettered only by Hammond and Washbrook. With seven hundreds and an average of 84.90 the great Hammond, though never consistently fit to play regularly, certainly ended his last full English season in style. Unable then to foretell what lay ahead, none of us then knew that Hammond was soon to embark on one tour too many.

Denis headed the Middlesex batting in championship games with, predictably, Bill Edrich second and Jack Robertson third. In all his first-class matches Jack got more than 2,000 runs, to begin a notable sequence of consistent success.

In his *Playing for England*, Denis set out the terms of the three-year contract he signed with Middlesex before the season began; £6 a week throughout the year, another £8 a match during the summer and all expenses paid. For playing in the Test series he received £36 per match.

61

That was the going rate at the time against India, New Zealand and West Indies. For Test matches against South Africa or Australia, which were played over a longer duration, the fee was £60. Professional cricketers – and their counterparts in football – might look enviously in those days at what the top golfers and a few tennis players were earning. No doubt they still can, the affluent times for tennis players having arrived for more than a quorum.

1946/47: His First Tour of Australia

O N AUGUST 31 1946 Denis set sail on the *Stirling Castle* for his first overseas tour, to Australia and New Zealand. English cricket, so soon after the war, was not yet ready to challenge Australia on equal terms, but MCC rightly agreed with their oldest opponents that their traditional rivalry should be resumed at the earliest opportunity. Walter Hammond's team were to lose the Test series 3–0 – better at least than the fate of J. W. H. T. Douglas's side which went out to resume battle after the Great War. That one suffered a whitewash.

MCC's batting, headed in the first four Tests by Len Hutton, Cyril Washbrook, Bill Edrich, Compton and Hammond, looked formidable enough but fears about their bowling strength proved abundantly justified. Much depended on Alec Bedser and Doug Wright; both of them consequently were overworked. England's fortunes were not helped by the arrival on the Test match scene of one of the outstanding fast bowling combinations, Ray Lindwall and Keith Miller, who were supported by Ernie Toshack, an accurate, nagging left-armer of medium pace, as well as spinners of such variety and quality as Colin McCool, George Tribe, Bruce Dooland and Ian Johnson. The Australians' batting was equally formidable; Don Bradman, Lindsay Hassett and Sidney Barnes, three Australian survivors from their 1938 side, were now supported by the left-handed opener, Arthur Morris, who made a considerable impact in the series.

The England batting, which stood no chance on a brute of a pitch in the first Test, never quite delivered the goods. Hammond, a 'loner' by nature and consequently a distant captain, began the tour in the old imperious form but in his four Test matches he failed to get past 32. An attack of fibrositis obliged him to stand down in the last Test. Hutton, too, had health problems.

Denis made no great contributions to the first three matches of the series but still finished it averaging more than 50. In all first-class matches on the tour Denis made 1,660 runs. Yet, as E. W. Swanton observed, he did not, except on a few memorable occasions, play quite as well as he could have. Hammond wanted his batsmen to play the spinners *his* way, from the crease. Such tactics were anathema to Denis.

There was little wrong with Denis's form at the beginning when MCC spent the first three weeks of the tour in Western Australia. Those players used to hectic modern touring schedules may note the leisurely difference with envy.

He tuned up with 84 in a two-day game against a Country Districts side, stood down from the fixture against Western Australia, in which Hammond made 208, and then got 97 against a Combined XI before sallying forth to a leg-break from Dooland and getting stumped. From Perth, MCC made the long railway journey across the barren Nullarbor plain to Adelaide.

Another two-day encounter with an S. A. Country XI brought Denis exactly 100 in sixty-seven minutes. This was followed by a lively 71 when MCC occupied two days in making 506 for five declared on a benign pitch against South Australia. They could not quite force a victory, but hundreds by Hutton and Washbrook, and 71 by Edrich, were reassuring with the first Test not so far away.

There was further encouragement in Melbourne where they defeated Victoria by 244 runs but, as it turned out, this was to be their only first-class victory in Australia. In the first innings Denis was at his best with 143 made in just three hours. In the second, Hutton shone just as brilliantly with 151 not out in fifty minutes more. Denis settled for 18 when he went in again. He was not to rediscover the magic touch until two months later, in Tasmania, just before the fourth Test match.

The next fixture, against an Australian XI in Melbourne, gave MCC their first sight of Bradman on this tour. He duly obliged them by making 106, although a missed stumping off Denis by Godfrey Evans when Bradman was on 78 may have contributed to Evans's omission from the England side in the first Test, in favour of Paul Gibb. Evans didn't let the selectors down for the rest of the series after they had selected him for the next Test. I should also add that Arthur Morris introduced himself to MCC with 115, and that Denis got 24 before being stumped off McCool. Hammond, coming in next, would not have approved.

MCC next moved on to Sydney where, in a match against New South Wales ruined by rain, Hutton ran himself out for 97 when seeking to face the last over. In their last match before the first Test, MCC played an unimpressive draw with Queensland, relying on Washbrook and Edrich to save face. Denis got 55 and 13, his finest touch still missing.

Australia had known in earlier days what it was like to bat at Brisbane after the Woolloongabba pitch had been flooded by the rains. It was

England's misfortune to suffer the experience on this tour, as they were to do again four years later. They lost the toss, saw Australia make 645, and then, after the heavens opened, were defeated by the huge margin of an innings and 332 runs with a day to spare. (The Tests in this series were scheduled to last for six days, with five hours of play in each.)

It is part of cricket's lore that Bradman, now playing his first Test match for eight years, and making a distinctly uncertain start, had struggled to reach 28 when England thought they had him caught by Jack Ikin fielding at slip to Bill Voce. Denis, fielding at long leg, was sure the ball had carried. Bedser thinks Bradman had every right to await the umpire's verdict but considers that it was not a bump ball. Keith Miller, playing in his first Test match, and due in next, grabbed his bat and gloves and was on his way, so certain was he from his position in the pavilion that Bradman was out. But the umpire did not think so, and that is all that mattered. From that point, as Miller recalls, the two captains resumed a state of war.

Bradman went on to get 187, and Lindsay Hassett also made a hundred. England dropped several catches in the innings. By the end of the third day England were 21 for the loss of Hutton, clean bowled by Miller. That evening, the storm broke, hailstones beating a cacophony on the old pavilion's tin roof.

On the fourth day England did well to reach 117 for five before the rains came down again. On the fifth, on an increasingly evil pitch, their last fifteen wickets went down in three and a half hours. They were bowled out for 141 and 172, Miller taking seven for 60 in the first innings and Toshack six for 82 in the second. England's batsmen resisted with skill and courage in a hopeless cause. Denis made 17 and 15, being lbw to Miller in one innings and caught at short leg off Toshack in the other.

Although the second Test, in Sydney, went into a sixth and final day, England slumped yet again to an innings defeat, this time by 33 runs. They paid the price, after Hammond had won the toss, for an inadequate first innings of 255 to which Australia replied with another massive total, 659 for eight declared. Barnes and Bradman, each of them making 234, shared a partnership of 405 for the third wicket which still remains a world Test record.

England did creditably enough by getting 371 in their second innings. Denis made 5 and 54, being dismissed on each occasion in an unfortunate fashion. In one innings he was caught by the wicket keeper, Don

Tallon, off a rebound from slip. In the other, Bradman at slip somehow held on to a catch after the ball had been cushioned between his thighs.

MCC's morale at this stage of the tour was at a low ebb. Their first innings in the second Test was even more disappointing in that Ray Lindwall was missing from Australia's attack. Most comfort lay in the batting of Edrich, whose 71 and 119 put to rest, once and for all, unworthy suspicions that he lacked the Test match temperament. Doug Wright had figures of one for 169, a travesty of his true worth, while the Victorian off-spinner, Ian Johnson, took eleven wickets.

In this Test, as Ian Peebles has related, Denis was bowling to Bradman as he neared 200. Hammond told him to keep the Don quiet by bowling wide of the off stump to a predominantly offside field. Despite this tactic the leg side boundary continued to be lashed. 'What did I tell you?' an incensed captain enquired. 'I heard you, skipper,' Denis said, 'and I haven't yet pitched one less than two feet wide of the off peg.' Denis remained staunchly loyal to his skipper, his admiration for Hammond's gifts as a player unbounded, but along with many others found it difficult to establish a close and warm relationship.

Before the series was continued in Melbourne on New Year's Day, Denis had two country engagements in New South Wales, and no doubt felt more cheerful after making 75 not out in one of them and 76 in the other in his most carefree style.

In the third Test England stopped the rot by hanging out for a draw. English prospects looked pleasing on the first day when Australia were reduced to 192 for six but two bowlers, Voce and Edrich, went lame and the attack had to be borne, staunchly enough, by Bedser, Wright and Yardley. A not-out hundred by McCool carried Australia to a total of 365.

England in their turn made 351, Edrich playing a pugnacious innings of 89 before he was given out lbw to Lindwall after getting an apparent inside edge. Shortly afterwards Denis pushed forward to the left armer Toshack, who was bowling over the wicket, without playing a shot and was adjudged in similar terms. Surprised by the decision, and clearly thinking that the ball had pitched outside his leg stump, Denis quite uncharacteristically – and I think for the only time in his career – waited for a second or two before walking. This sparked off controversy in the Australian press. Washbrook, however, who was batting with Denis at the time, said later that he thought it was a fair decision.

Australia scored 536 in their second innings, with Morris making 155, Lindwall 100 and Tallon 92, the last two assaulting England's bowling in an eighth wicket partnership of 154. That left England seven hours to play out time which, thanks chiefly to Washbrook (112) and Yardley (53 not out), they managed to do, scoring 310 for seven.

Denis in this last innings was run out for 14 after hitting a ball wide of Miller in the covers and setting off for a single while Washbrook remained rooted behind the crease. Unfortunately, Denis did not call and his partner did not back up.

Having failed, at this stage of the tour, to get past 50 more than twice in his last eleven innings, Denis badly needed something to re-charge his batteries. MCC's visit to Tasmania provided a timely opportunity. In his second innings against a strong Combined XI in Hobart, he enthralled the islanders with 124 in less than two hours. Then, in his only knock against Tasmania at Launceston he got 163 in just under three hours.

In the fourth Test at Adelaide, Denis at last put his stamp on the series by scoring a hundred in each innings, making it four centuries in a row. It was warm work; the temperature hovered above the 100 mark throughout. 'It was the hottest Test I ever played in,' Keith Miller recalls, 'and it was difficult to sleep at night. There was no air-conditioning in those days.'

Two hours and a quarter for his first 43 runs in the first innings illustrates how hard Denis had to struggle against a field that was set back defensively to test his patience. But he hit his stride by mid-afternoon on the second day and played with much brilliance after he had completed his century. England made what was comfortably their highest total of the series, 460, with Denis scoring 147 and Hutton 94.

Australia in their turn got 487 in which Morris made his second consecutive Test hundred and Miller hit 141 not out. So far, only a slight advantage to Australia but despite another century opening partnership by Hutton and Washbrook (their third in a row), there came a time when England stood on 255 for eight, only 228 runs ahead. Denis firmly held one end, but he was running out of partners.

At this critical point Godfrey Evans came out to join him in an unbroken partnership of 85 which enabled Hammond to declare and ensured a draw. It is very well known that Evans resisted for 97 minutes before getting off the mark, largely because Denis, with remarkable patience and concentration, so effectively farmed the strike that his partner rarely received more than two balls in succession.

'Bradman had his field set right back for Denis,' Godfrey remembers, 'and we walked singles off the fifth or sixth in an eight-ball over. But he had his bees round the honey pot when I had the strike.' He also remembers Keith Miller bowling a nasty bouncer at Denis which rose head high. Denis, right behind the line, played it down off his eyebrows. 'They don't,' Keith said, 'come any better than this bugger, do they?'

England eventually closed their second innings at 340 for eight, whereupon Australia brought matters to a quiet conclusion by making 215 for one. Arthur Morris followed Denis's example by making his second hundred in the match. I might add by way of postscript that Bradman in his first innings was bowled by Bedser for 0, that Australia, with one Test still to play, had already won the series, and that Arthur Morris, himself one of the most charming of men, has supplied me with as glowing a tribute to Denis as any that I have come by. 'He was a wonderful person to be with, both on and off the field. His attitude was what all of us like to believe epitomises the game of cricket.'

The English players then travelled from Adelaide to Melbourne by air, the first flight made by an MCC side in Australia. Denis followed a 61 in a Country frolic with all but a fifth successive first-class hundred, against Victoria. He had got 93 in his most effervescent style when Miller made a testing return catch look a simple matter.

In the last State game, the return fixture with New South Wales, he scored 75 and 74 not out. He and Hutton had an unfinished stand of 127 in one hour, an episode reported by E. W. Swanton as being the most scintillating of the tour. 'There have been relatively few Hutton – Compton partnerships, but those there have been remain memorable, for each seems to bring the very best out of the other.'

England lost the final Test in Sydney, by five wickets, but it was a good match of cricket and they had their hopeful moments, not least when Doug Wright took seven for 105 to bowl out Australia for 253. England scored 280 and led on first innings for the only time in the series, Hutton having retired ill on 122, his first Test hundred in Australia. He was later sent to hospital with tonsillitis and a high temperature, and took no further part. Denis made 17, hit wicket bowled Lindwall when going back a shade too far in fending down a short one. He always made generous use of the crease when playing back.

When England batted again they knew that something around 250 could be enough on a wearing pitch. Denis held the innings together with 76 before he was taken in Toshack's leg trap, but the final total, 186, was not sufficient to prevent Australia from winning their third victory with a day to spare.

Norman Yardley took over as England's captain in this Test. It so happened that in all his first-class matches under his leadership Denis averaged exactly 90 whereas under that of Hammond he managed less than 40 – and that included 250 runs for once out in the Adelaide Test. He was to attain a similar average, under Yardley again, in the following English summer.

Before all that, however, MCC flew on to New Zealand where Denis got 38 in the Test match at Christchurch and, in the last fixture of the tour against Auckland, 97 not out and eleven wickets for 49 on a turning pitch. This impressive match analysis enabled him to head the overall tour bowling averages with some ease.

The MCC party flew back to Sydney, and thence on to London in four separate parties. Some remarkable events lay not very far ahead.

1947: The Golden Summer

1947 WAS, FOR DENIS, the most successful English season that any batsman has enjoyed. Although he began with an impressive 73 for MCC against Yorkshire on a drying pitch, in his next seven innings he got past 50 just once. There was no hint yet of what was to come. But he then took 97 off the touring South Africans in another innings for MCC, missing a hundred only when losing patience against an attack operating to a generous width. That really got him going, and his form for the next five weeks was simply irresistible.

His next scores in an exceptional sequence were 88 not out and 112 for Middlesex against Worcestershire. At one stage in his second innings he advanced down the pitch against the leg-spinner, Roly Jenkins, while that engaging character was still in the middle of his approach. Declining to deliver, Roly said, 'I don't mind you giving me the charge, Denis, but am I expected to shake you by the hand?'

In his next match, Middlesex v Sussex, Denis made 110 in his only innings, sharing in a stand of 223 with Bill Edrich. On six occasions in this season, Compton and Edrich had partnerships of more than 200.

When the South Africans returned to Lord's for the county game, Denis made it three centuries in a row with a flawless 154 in his first innings. It says something for the accuracy of the Springbok spinners, Athol Rowan and Tufty Mann, that the innings took four hours, quite slow scoring by Compton's standards. He always had a high regard for Rowan, who took his wicket twice in this match, bowling him for 34 in the second innings in which Edrich's 133 not out was crucial in saving the game on a wearing pitch.

That 34 was his only score of less than 50 in eleven successive innings. Next came 88 against Hampshire. In this match Jack Robertson registered his first double century and he and Denis made 193 together in about an hour and a half. Middlesex, declaring at 429 for six, still had time enough on the first evening to grab a Hampshire wicket. All this was exactly in line with Walter Robins's requirement as his side advanced towards their first championship title since 1921.

It was time now for the start of a new Test series against South Africa, captained by Alan Melville. Melville's men relished the opportunity to prove themselves at international level for the first time since 1938/39. Those of us old enough to remember the 1947 cricket season like to recall it as one of uninterrupted sunshine, the best season, weatherwise, since the war. It certainly had the most lovely climax. But the fact was that it snowed at Worcester during the South African's first fixture, the third Test was played in some nasty weather at the beginning of July and the fourth, at the end of that month, was also affected by the weather.

The touring side found themselves leaning heavily on the old guard – Melville, Bruce Mitchell and Dudley Nourse – while their new batsmen adjusted themselves to damp pitches in the early part of the tour. Test matches apart, they were to win eleven and draw six of their last seventeen first-class matches when pitches became almost uniformly firm. In the Test series when, for the first time in England, South Africa had four days scheduled for each match, they were to lose three and draw two. They might well have wondered afterwards just what the result of the rubber would have been had England been denied the services of just one of the pair the Springboks dubbed 'the terrible twins'.

There was no question which side held the initiative in a drawn first Test, at Trent Bridge. South Africa capitalised on the toss to score 533 (Melville 189, Nourse 149) and promptly bowled out England for 208 on a pitch then typically a good deal more benign than some of those now seen at Trent Bridge. Edrich and Compton, 57 and 65 respectively, were England's top scorers. Denis was caught at slip off the second new ball.

In the follow-on, a long, long way behind, England at one moment had lost four wickets for 170, with another 155 runs needed to save themselves from an innings defeat, when Norman Yardley, their last specialist batsman, now joined Denis. Their forthright answer to this crisis was to make 237 for the fifth wicket, an England record against South Africa. Yardley made 99, Denis a quite faultless 163 in four and three-quarter hours, and Godfrey Evans weighed in with 74 in even time.

England made 551 in their second innings, after which South Africa quietly played out time, at 166 for one. Alan Melville scored two centuries in the match. Denis's feat of getting a hundred in his first Test match against South Africa repeated his achievements, before the war, against both Australia and the West Indies. Denis has always said that he could hardly go wrong when Yardley was his captain. Further evidence of this was to be forthcoming in 1948.

By this stage of the summer Middlesex looked to be running away with the championship but, after seven wins in a row, they were held to a draw by Yorkshire in a rain-affected match at Lord's. Denis had made a sparkling 50 not out in his one innings.

It ought to be added here that Bill Edrich's form, if less arresting than that of Denis, was quite remarkably consistent. The time seemed ripe for something special from the pair of them when the second Test was played on their own pitch. They obliged their faithful supporters with a stand of 370 for the third wicket, which was then a world Test record. Edrich made 189, Denis 208, his highest Test innings so far. Long before the end of their partnership they were doing much as they pleased, Edrich thumping the ball away on the leg side and Denis indulging his love for the sweep as well as making cover point's life a misery.

England scored 554 for eight declared and required South Africa (327) to follow on. The tourists were bowled out again for 252 and went down by ten wickets. Doug Wright had a splendid match with his leg-breaks, taking five wickets in each innings. Edrich, opening England's attack with Bedser, and hurling himself into the task with characteristic zeal, took three for 31 in the second innings. Denis, bowling in his old orthodox style, took four for 78 off 52 overs all told. Not a bad all-round performance by the Middlesex duo.

At one point during the record partnership the Springbok spinners held a tactical discussion. 'How can we stop Denis giving us the charge?' Athol Rowan asked, 'What about bowling it over his head?' Tufty Mann suggested. 'Well, it's your idea, Tufty, you try it.' So Tufty did, whereupon Denis stopped in his tracks and with an overhead tennis smash struck him past cover for four. 'If I had had to earn my living bowling to Denis,' Athol now reflects, 'I'd have retired prematurely, destitute and unsuccessful.'

The 208 he scored in the second Test brought Denis's first dazzling sequence of the summer to an end: eleven innings, five hundreds, an average of 129. Yorkshire's bowlers then brought him down to earth, in Bill Bowes's benefit match at Headingley, by dismissing him for 4 and 15 on a nasty rain-affected pitch. Two innings by Bill Edrich, 70 and 102, were supreme examples of his battling spirit. Denis took seven wickets for 51, and Middlesex won inside two days.

Denis played in one further game before the third Test, MCC against Cambridge University at Lord's, a two-day affair not designated as first-class. It seems worth a passing mention since he failed twice more, scoring 3 and 1. P. B. Datta, a freshman from Calcutta, and M. R. G.

72

Left: *Textbook batting stance in Denis's 'teens*

Bottom: *Indian Gymkhana CC and a Middlesex County XI at Osterley in July 1935. Middlesex players are (top row) W. R. Watkins (second left), J. A. Young (second right); (standing) Jim Bailey, Colin Fairservice (second and third left), Laurie Gray (fifth left); (in front, l–r) F. Putner, A. E. Wilson, Denis Compton*

Below: *Going out to bat with Middlesex in 1937 with one of his heroes, Patsy Hendren. Patsy retired from cricket at the end of that season*

Top left: *War-time wedding day – to Doris, at St John's Wood Church, in March 1941*

Top right: *A drive (past cover point's right hand?) against Nottinghamshire in 1939*

Above: *Going out to bat with Andy Wilson on the day in 1947 when he passed Tom Hayward's aggregate record for an English season*

BRYLCREEM

for confident grooming

Men who hit the headlines know that smartness counts — and count on Brylcreem for perfect grooming. Brylcreem works in two ways — (1) It grooms without gumming, giving life and lustre to the hair. (2) The pure natural oils in Brylcreem are emulsified into a rich cream which, with massage, has a valuable tonic effect, preventing dry hair and dandruff. Brylcreem comes in tubs 1/8, 2/6 and 4/6, or handy tubes 2/6.

BRYLCREEM — the perfect hairdressing

royds 69 1

A well-remembered advertisement – and no need to identify the face under remarkably well-groomed hair

'And this is how it should be done' – a demonstration for young soccer admirers at Hendon in November 1947

Opposite left: *Driving off the last tee for Arsenal in November 1948 – another ball game that always came easily to Denis, with a swing both sweet and smooth*

Opposite right: *Denis and brother Leslie ('Big Les') with the FA Cup won by Arsenal in 1950*

Arsenal took time off for golf when they trained at Brighton before the FA Cup final in 1950. Left to right: Ian McPherson, Denis, Walley Barnes, and Doug Lishman

Opposite: *The Arsenal team which defeated Liverpool in the 1950 FA Cup final. Left to right: (standing) Tom Whittaker (manager), Laurie Scott, George Swindin, Walley Barnes; (seated) Denis, Peter Goring, Alex Forbes, Joe Mercer (captain), Reg Lewis, Leslie Compton; (in front) Jimmy Logie, Freddie Cox*

Opposite left: *The celebrated 'Middlesex twins' going out to bat for Middlesex in their* annus mirabilis, *1947*

Opposite right: *Denis, an unwilling spectator at Lord's, after an operation on that knee in 1950*

Opposite below: *Caught by Keith Miller off Ray Lindwall in the fifth Test at Melbourne in 1950/51. Denis had no joy in this series, but this was the Test which provided England with a victory over Australia for the first time after the second World War*

Right: *The hook shot – a superb illustration of technique, in one of the best action pictures ever taken*

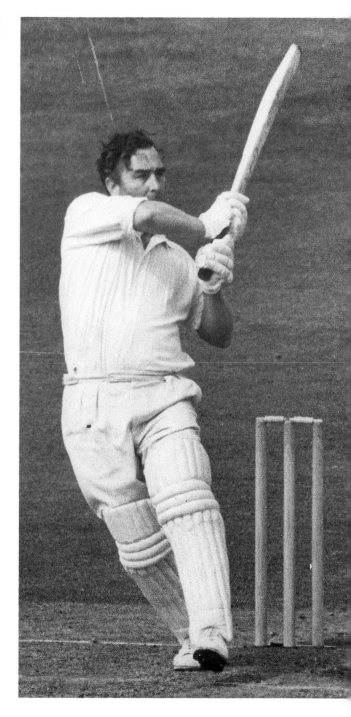

Above: *Four or six? Dick Howorth has been despatched to – or over – the mid-wicket boundary in the Middlesex–Worcestershire game at Lord's in May 1951, when he was not far off from scoring 1,000 runs before the end of the month*

Left: *Pictured at Southampton when returning from South Africa in January 1952 with his second wife, Valerie*

Earls-Davis deserve some kindos, in this of all seasons, for taking his wicket so cheaply.

Within a few days he and Edrich were renewing their assault on South Africa's bowlers and Denis embarked on a second triumphant sequence of scores, with scarcely a hiccough along the way, which was to last from early July until the middle of September.

He began it with his third successive Test hundred and his best innings in the series. The fact that it was played on an unpleasant pitch is not apparent from bare figures which reveal that Edrich and Compton put on 228 for the third England wicket in only three hours and ten minutes.

Having completed his second 50 in an hour, Denis got out for 115. Edrich, after pull-driving the new ball for three huge sixes, went on to make 191, and England replied with 478 to South Africa's 339. Although Dudley Nourse subsequently hit the finest of his Test hundreds, South Africa were bowled out again for 267 and England, winning by seven wickets, went dormy two in the series. Bill Edrich, 22 not out, was in at the death having scarcely left the field throughout the four days. As the spearhead of England's attack he bowled all but fifty-eight overs and took eight wickets.

After two days of rest from these labours he and Denis, for Middlesex at Leicester, rattled up yet another double century stand, 277, in two hours and ten minutes. Having made his hundred in even time, Denis contented himself with 151. Edrich, who captained the side for the first time since turning amateur in the spring, got 257. Later, when Middlesex needed 66 to win in twenty-five minutes, they went in first to get the runs off seven overs with four minutes in hand. For decent measure, Denis took five for 108 in Leicestershire's second innings.

Of the seventeen first-class matches which Denis played in July, August and September there were only two on which he failed to make an exciting imprint. One of these, Gentlemen v Players, which remained an important fixture, came next in his programme. Trevor Bailey had him caught behind by Billy Griffith for 11. The great New Zealander left-hander, Martin Donnelly, then captain of Oxford, scored a thrilling 162.

In the following game, Middlesex v Essex at Lord's, Trevor Bailey was imprudent enough to stand too close at silly-mid-off for Peter Smith's leg-breaks and googlies while Denis was busy making 129 in two hours. He needed eight stitches in the webbing between the third and little finger of his left hand, and had them taped together for the rest of his career. The Essex skipper, Tom Pearce, remembers that he reinforced the off side with an additional extra cover. 'Much good did it do us. Denis still hit the ball through them, just where he wanted.'

The story about Denis and his rare use of the straight drive now crops up again. According to Doug Insole, who was then in his first season for Essex, Ray Smith said to Denis at the tea interval, 'We seem to have seen everything except the straight drive.' 'OK,' Denis replied. 'If you're on, first over after tea.' Ray Smith was. His first ball disappeared into the pavilion enclosure by the sightscreen.

I am tolerably certain, as previously indicated, that Denis was challenged to play this shot on more than one occasion. Several members of the Middlesex camp allege that it was Walter Robins who inspired him to show what he could do in this respect, in another game altogether.

The Northants captain had a similar experience to his Essex counterpart in the next match when Denis got 110 and Edrich 267 not out, the two of them making 211 together, their fourth 'doubleton' partnership of the summer. It was the highest score of Edrich's career. And, for goodly measure yet again, Denis took six for 78 and three for 100.

England's victory, by ten wickets, in the fourth Test at Headingley now gave them a winning 3–0 lead in the series. It was the only one of eight matches Denis played against the Springboks that summer in which he did not get a hundred, but the 30 he got on a damp pitch was no cause for self-approach. The fact was, though, that at this point in his career his highest score in Yorkshire remained the 51 he had made on his first visit there, in 1936.

England's third success in a row was largely made possible by an opening stand of 141 between Hutton and Washbrook which later enabled Yardley to declare at 317 for seven with a first innings lead of 142. Thus far it had been a thin series for Hutton but now, in his first Test match on his home turf, he made a faultless 100. South Africa's second innings, 184, was not substantial enough to set England anything but the most comfortable target. The Lancashire captain, Ken Cranston, finished it off with four wickets for no runs in one over, after Denis had held a stunning left-handed catch at short extra to dismiss Melville off Young's bowling.

The month of August began with Denis having made 2,071 runs at an average of 76, and Edrich 2,358 at a yet dizzier 107. These figures were improved as Denis scored his tenth hundred of the summer, 100 not out, and Edrich got 76 and 54 not out in James Langridge's benefit match at Hove. Middlesex made one of their first-day declarations, 401 for four at 85 runs per hour.

At Canterbury, Kent made Denis work harder for another hundred, 106, but normal service was restored at The Oval where Middlesex scored 537 for two on the first day against Surrey. Their score card read: Brown 98, Robertson 127, Edrich 157 not out, Compton 137 not out. The two last named hit 287 in two and three-quarter hours, after which Denis, with his new-style back of the hand bowling, took six for 94 and six for 80. In figures, at least, this was the best all-round performance of his career. The Oval gates were closed by 3 o'clock on the Saturday, with 30,000 spectators inside the ground.

Middlesex now returned to Lord's for the return match with Kent and an innings by Denis that I and everyone else lucky enough to witness it will never forget. Bryan Valentine, the Kent skipper, set Middlesex 397 to win on the third day at more than 90 runs an hour. They went down, in the end, by 75 runs but while Denis held sway, batting with total mastery and superb elan against Doug Wright, who was at his best, all things seemed possible.

George Mann got out for 57 after he had assisted the maestro to add 161 in little more than an hour and a half, and Denis eventually went for 168, having made his last 71 runs in forty minutes with a riveting mix of orthodox and improvised strokes. I still think of it as the most thrilling innings I saw him play, and he himself will say modestly that he doubts if he ever played better, and certainly not in a losing cause.

Mann recalls it as the most amazing innings he ever saw at close quarters. 'I remember two shots especially: one a tennis-like top-spin flick, against Wright, over the head of short leg and then, when Fred Ridgway took the new ball without anyone at slip, Denis deliberately steered him through the first slip area off the face of his bat.'

Valentine did not make the mistake of splitting his field, but he had to set a defensive one. Les Ames found himself at fly slip, half way back towards third man. 'Denis seemed a bit piqued by this, but it didn't make any difference. He was unstoppable. It has to be one of the greatest innings I can remember.'

Gubby Allen watched it from the committee room. 'I've never seen footwork like it. Doug Wright was bowling on or outside the leg stump to an on-side field but Denis still hit him through the empty spaces on the off. It was tremendous.' Jack Robertson recalls that as Denis unrolled one hundred after another that season they thought, 'Well, this has to be the best so far. And then he would go one better. But we didn't see how he could improve on this one.'

This memorable hundred against Kent was Denis's thirteenth of the summer. He still had seven matches to play, so by now it was clear that the records of Jack Hobbs and Tom Hayward were within his reach. I dare say he became aware of the possibilities only by reading the papers. By this time, certainly, he was seeing the ball so well that he might have batted with one eye closed and with the proverbial stick of rhubarb.

In the first innings of the final Test match at The Oval he got 53. In the second, wearing plimsolls, he scored a radiant 113, in a mere hour and three-quarters, to close within two of Hobbs's sixteen hundreds. These scores brought him to an aggregate for the series of 753 at an average of 94.12.

A high-scoring match was drawn, South Africa taking a full share of the honours by making 423 for seven in the last innings, only 28 short of victory. England got 427 and 325 for six declared, South Africa in their first innings 302. Bruce Mitchell, 120 and 189 not out, became the second South African batsman in the series to hit two hundreds in one match. The Test was played in a heatwave, Hubert Preston recording in *Wisden* that '26,980 spectators assembled on Monday, the sun blazing down on the compact mass of people in the lightest permissible summer attire.'

Middlesex at this time had three championship games left, all of them at Lord's. In the first, against Surrey, Denis made 178 in his first innings, enjoying a partnership of 304 with George Mann which lasted for three hours and a quarter, and 19 not out in his second. He now needed one more hundred to equal the sixteen scored by Jack Hobbs in 1925, and Middlesex needed one more victory to be certain of winning the championship. Denis got 60 and 85 on a wearing pitch against Northamptonshire and it was utterly in character that with a declaration looming in the second innings he should have been bowled by Vince Broderick when having a dip. Middlesex won by 355 runs to clinch the county title.

The media now had an obviously exciting story for its spotlight and every cricketer worth his salt focused attention on the Middlesex-Lancashire game at Lord's. On the first day, while Denis was fielding, the story became more dramatic: his right knee 'locked' so badly that Bill Tucker, the distinguished orthopaedic surgeon (and former England Rugby international), conducted a manipulative operation in the pavilion. This was successful enough for Denis to play a full part in the game after the week-end. In his first innings he made only 17 but in his second, amidst scenes of mounting excitement, he drew level with Jack Hobbs's record after spending the best part of half an hour in the 90s. Denis, who went on to score 139, has said that he thought this was the only selfish innings he played. Yet he was surely entitled to take his time; his side was fighting, unsuccessfully, to avoid defeat.

So to the grand climax at the Hastings festival where in his first match, for South of England against the South Africans, he went past Hobbs to set a record that may never be surpassed. When he reached 101 (out of 151) the ovation lasted for five minutes. Walter Robins and Bill Edrich came out to join in the congratulations. First ball after the resumption, he gave his wicket away, stumped off 'Tufty' Mann. Trevor Bailey remembers being in with him when the milestone was passed. 'I was worried stiff that I might run him out.'

Making 30 in the second innings of this match, Denis now had Tom Hayward's aggregate (3,518 in 1906) well within his sights. He needed another 132 runs when playing his second festival game, for the South of England against Sir Pelham Warner's XI. The deed was done with scores of 87 not out and 86. The runs were hard earned, with no one else on his side getting past 50. Andy Wilson remembers going out to bat with him in the morning. 'Denis seemed totally unconcerned about the record he was about to break. All he talked about was the time I put him on to bowl for the Young Professionals at Lord's way back in the thirties.'

One match remained, Middlesex (then county champions) against the Rest of England at The Oval. In this match Denis, in spite of the limitations imposed by a heavily strapped knee, not yet fully recovered from the breakdown against Lancashire, finished his *annus mirabilis* in a blaze of glory. So, suitably enough, did Edrich, whose 180 also enabled him to beat Hayward's previous record. Denis made 246, his highest score to date in England and an innings that was interrupted on the first day for running repairs to the knee.

The most memorable stroke he played, in a stand with Edrich that eventually reached 210, occurred when he went down the pitch to Tom Goddard, fell flat on his face yet still managed to sweep the ball for four off the middle of the bat. 'One of these days,' the Gloucestershire off-spinner said, 'there'll be no bloody return ticket.' It was several years, I think, before Denis missed out when giving him the charge again. 'Got you at last,' Tom roared, before bringing out of his pocket a single ticket, outward half only.

Denis ended his season with eighteen hundreds, 3,816 runs and an average of 90.85. Bill Edrich – twelve hundreds, 3,539 runs – stood second in the averages on 80.43. Jack Robertson also got twelve hundreds in all first class matches. Both he and Denis were missing from the Middlesex side during the fifth Test match when they won a crucial encounter against Gloucestershire, the eventual runners-up, at Cheltenham. Middlesex became the first southern county to take the title since they themselves had done so twenty-six years earlier. Of their twenty-six championship matches they won nineteen, lost five and drew just two. Of the thirty-seven hundreds made by their batsmen in the County Championship Denis (11), Robertson (11) and Edrich (8) had a king-sized share. In all first-class matches the first four in their batting order – Brown, Robertson, Edrich and Compton – totalled more than 12,000 runs. Between mid-May 1946 and mid-September 1947 Denis scored *thirty-three* hundreds. I must not omit to mention that by the end of July Bill Edrich had taken 67 wickets at an average of 22. But for a shoulder strain, which stopped him bowling again that summer, he might well have equalled J. H. Parks's record, achieved the year before, of 3,000 runs and 100 wickets in a season.

Denis has said that all the runs he made in his marvellous summer of 1947, including six hundreds off South African bowling, were made with the same narrow-grained Warsop bat. This claim, coming as it does from someone who could never be relied on to have all the essential equipment with him, should perhaps be taken with a pinch of salt. But I believe the bat was still going strong several years later.

At the end of a cricket season which was estimated to have attracted a total audience of almost three million, Denis was presented by Sir Pelham Warner with a silver salver commemorating his seventeenth hundred, and the Hendon council gave a dinner in his honour. The cricket world, the whole sporting world, it seemed, lay at the feet of a modest, unassuming hero whose fame and popularity not even Gordon Richards or Stanley Matthews could outdo. He now went back to Highbury to earn himself a League winners' medal with Arsenal and, in due course, MCC sent out an inadequate side to cope with the three W's in the Caribbean.

1948: Two Memorable Hundreds Against Australia

NO ONE COULD HAVE EXPECTED Denis to follow the *tour de force* of 1947 with something quite so extraordinary. He contented himself in 1948 with a mere eight hundreds of which two, still recalled with admiration by those who witnessed them, were made in the Test series against what was arguably the best side in the entire history of cricket.

The tour of Don Bradman's Australians, which marked the end of the road for the greatest run-maker the game has ever known, turned out to be one of almost uninterrupted triumph. They became the first visiting team in England to go through their entire programme unbeaten; indeed, they won half of their games by an innings. And, although Bradman lost four out of five tosses in the rubber, they also became the first combination to win four out of five Test matches on English soil.

Seven Australians, headed by the Don himself (2,428) and Arthur Morris (1,922), made more than one thousand runs. Their batting was so strong that Bill Brown, who scored eight first-class hundreds, could find a place in only two of the Tests. But it was their bowling which gave them the most crucial advantage.

Ray Lindwall and Keith Miller were at their peak. The gangling Bill Johnston, left arm over the wicket, took as many wickets (27) in the Tests as Lindwall, and another left-armer, the medium-paced Ernie Toshack, came on as second change to keep things tight until another new ball became due. An experimental rule providing a new ball after fifty-five overs simply played into Australia's hands.

With inadequate support for Alec Bedser at the other end, England could not begin to match the quality of Australia's seam attack while their batting, although it began promisingly with the names of Hutton, Washbrook, Edrich and Compton, had nothing like the depth of their opponents. In spite of all this, England looked poised to win the third Test, at Old Trafford, when the weather took a decisive hand, and they certainly ought to have won the fourth, at Headingley, where they paid a high price for missing their chances in the field on the last day.

Denis began and ended his season with an impressive flourish. In between, however, his form was inconsistent. In May there was a fine

123, made in two hours for MCC against Surrey. For Middlesex, he made 94 against Worcestershire and 84 against Leicestershire, and, for MCC again, 26 and 20 in his first joust with the Australians. It seemed no happy augury that with a supposedly good batting side MCC should go down by an innings and 158 runs.

But the high point for Denis in May had been reached in his previous county game when he and Bill Edrich plundered Somerset's attack at Lord's in a third wicket partnership of 424, in just four hours, which still stands as an English record. His share in this was 252 not out, then the highest score of his career. Walter Robins, who played under Mann that season, must have approved of the general tempo, not least when the duo made 209 in seventy minutes after tea. Denis's share of those runs was 139. His final tally included three sixes and thirty-seven fours. Edrich had reached 168 when George Mann declared at 478 for two with fifty minutes of play still remaining, time enough for Laurie Gray to shoot out Somerset's opening pair, one of them the redoubtable Harold Gimblett.

Years later, a young player in the Middlesex dressing room asked Bill Edrich, with tongue in cheek, how it was that the number 3 batsman had managed to score so slowly in that 1948 encounter. 'A chap called Miles Coope came on as fourth change to bowl leg-breaks,' Edrich explained. 'He went for 61 in six overs, and I never received a ball from him.'

In early June, Denis made 0 (c Cranston b Copson) in a rain-affected and not very useful Test trial, at Edgbaston, before getting 59 on a turning pitch against Yorkshire. This, as it were, was a useful net in the week of the first Test match, although it was not to be a series in which English skills against the spinners could be much advertised.

However, in damp and gloomy conditions at Trent Bridge, England's fate in the first Test was virtually sealed when they were bowled out in their first innings for 165. Keith Miller struck a resounding early blow for Australia by bowling Hutton for 3 and another later when disposing of Denis, in similar fashion, for 19. On a pitch freshened by rain England were reduced to 74 for eight before the Surrey twosome, Laker and Bedser, put a less miserable complexion on matters with a stand of 89. Bill Johnston had five for 36. In mid-innings Lindwall retired with a groin strain, and took no further part in the match as a bowler.

After Australia had replied with 509 (Bradman 138, Lindsay Hassett 137) England had only one objective in view and, thanks mainly to Denis, who played one of his bravest and most disciplined innings, they made a good fist of saving the game. Their hopes endured until shortly before lunch on the final day when, having fought for almost seven hours, through *ten* periods of play, Denis stood on 184. Godfrey Evans was proving to be just the partner he needed to hold Australia at bay. But at that point, in murky light, Denis changed his mind when Miller bowled him a distinctly nasty bouncer which got up higher than he expected. In seeking to avoid it he lost his balance and trod on his stumps.

The ovation he received as he returned to the pavilion may still be ringing in his ears. England, bowled out for 441, went down by eight wickets but not before the admirable Bedser had the pleasure of dismissing Bradman for the second time in the match, on this occasion for his first Test nought in England.

I might add that Bradman, with all the time in the world at his disposal, took four and three quarter hours for his 138. Left-arm spinner Jack Young had figures of 60–28–79–1 in the first Australian innings, and at one time sent down eleven successive maidens. All this was a good deal less dramatic than some later events. The fur flew on the penultimate day when Miller, by then shouldering the main burden of attack, and predictably rising to the occasion, let loose five bouncers at Hutton in eight balls.

That got the crowd going, my word it did. Hutton and Denis had a partnership of 111 which promised much but, by bowling Hutton for 74, Miller made the two greatest English scalps his exclusive preserve. Of all the all-rounders he has seen, Denis rates Miller as second only to Gary Sobers.

Before the second Test began at Lord's Denis made 145 in the Middlesex–Kent game on a demanding pitch. In the next Test, he further demonstrated his defensive skills as Australia went two up in the rubber with an even more conclusive victory, by 409 runs. This was the only occasion in the series when Bradman won the toss. His side had the rub of the green, weatherwise, but it should be added that Miller was unable to bowl at all.

Arthur Morris scored 105, the first of his three hundreds in the series, in Australia's first innings of 350. Bradman got a rather tentative 38 before Bedser had him caught off an inswinger by Hutton at short leg, an exact reprise of his two dismissals at Trent Bridge.

The pitch was lively and the light not always ideal as England replied with 215, Denis making their top score of 53 with due circumspection before Miller picked up a lovely slip catch off Johnston. When Australia batted again they made the most of a sunny Saturday and an accommodating pitch by running up a total of 460 for seven declared in which Sidney Barnes got a trenchant 141 and Bradman, denied a farewell hundred at Lord's, 89. Bedser had Bradman's wicket for the fifth successive time in the Test matches.

Bradman's declaration left England to make 596 or, more realistically, to hold out for nine hours. E. W. Swanton recalls, as I do, a blazing hook by Denis off Lindwall on the penultimate evening. But first thing next morning, having made 29, he aimed to drive Johnston square on the off side and Miller in the gully took another exciting catch. England succumbed for 186.

The most disquieting feature of the English effort in this Test was the form of Hutton (20 and 13) who looked strangely fallible and lacking in confidence. England's selectors decided to drop him from their side for the next Test match while he returned to Yorkshire, for whom he promptly made a hundred, away to Essex.

Briefly on tour with Middlesex, Denis followed two low scores with 100 not out at Derby where Albert Alderman, their opening batsman, was given a testimonial in his last season. A collection was being taken for him when Denis got out cheaply in his first innings. Still with his pads on, Denis insisted on grabbing a bucket and circling the boundary himself. Alderman thought this a lovely gesture by a lovely bloke.

Now to the third Test, at Old Trafford, and the innings of 145 not out which Denis has recalled as the one which probably gave him more satisfaction than any other. George Emmett, the cultured Gloucestershire batsman, took Hutton's place but when England batted first on a greenish pitch both he and Washbrook were gone with only 28 on the board. Denis then went in to join Edrich, and Lindwall was not sparing with his bouncer. One nasty ball hit Denis on his arm. He had made 4 when Lindwall let go an even faster, shorter one which he first intended to evade but, hearing no-ball called, changed his mind, went for the hook and got a top edge on to his forehead.

Blood streamed from a nasty wound as he staggered to the ground. He was eventually led off the field for stitches, and although still obviously groggy, insisted that he should resume at the fall of the next wicket. He was talked out of this, eventually going in again when the fifth wicket went down at 141. Let me report Denis's own version of the incident. 'It was my own fault. The ball was a bit quicker than I expected. If I'd got my head out of the way it would have gone for four over the wicket keeper's head.'

Having taken some net practice, which even Denis in such circumstances thought prudent, he reappeared on the field to an enormous welcome from the crowd and tentatively sought to find his bearings again as Lindwall gave him the full treatment. This was the only time in his career, he has admitted, that he was genuinely frightened. He found himself drawing away for several overs, but forced himself to get regularly into line. A crisis was bravely overcome and, although England were to lose their captain, Norman Yardley, for 22, Godfrey Evans (34) provided further support in a stand of 75 for the seventh wicket. At close of play England were 231 for seven, Denis well into the groove again.

Next day, after the new ball had been taken first thing, Bedser rose to the challenge by helping Denis to add 121 for the eighth wicket against a fierce spell of bowling by Lindwall. Weathering this successfully, they were 3 runs short of a new England record against Australia when Denis called his partner for a single after Bradman had misfielded at cover. Sam Loxton pounced and threw down the wicket with Bedser, no Carl Lewis, still a long way from home. 'One of those occasions,' Bedser reflects, 'when you've got to be a willing sacrifice.'

Jack Young went in at number 11 and was intercepted by Denis who had tactical advice in mind. By way of opening the conversation the articulate Jack, a great one for literary allusions, said, 'Doctor Livingstone, I presume?' Denis failed to grasp the point. 'No, don't worry,' he replied. 'Just play up the line.'

Denis carried out his bat for 145 not out, having been in for five hours and twenty minutes. It was not, understandably enough, entirely unblemished; he gave several chances or half chances to the Australian wicket keeper, Don Tallon. But of this hundred, and the other big one in the first Test, Norman Yardley says, 'They were quite magnificent efforts, full of everything: temperament, skill, above all a terrific display of guts. I can't remember a faster or more aggressive spell of bowling than Lindwall's when he was trying to break the Compton–Bedser stand.'

England made 363 in their first innings and thereafter held a clear initiative. They bowled out Australia for 221 and declared in their turn at 174 for three, Washbrook getting 85 not out and Denis collecting an understandable 0. But bad weather now intervened, and there was no play on the Monday or on the Tuesday morning. On a dead pitch Australia finished at 92 for one. England had to wait more than two years for their first post-war victory over them.

Denis had now made eight hundreds in ten Test matches, and no one other than Bradman had ever done that.

On his way back home from Manchester, Jack Young observed huge pictures of Denis Compton advertising Brylcreem, high above the concourse at Euston Station. Each one was adorned with a newspaper across his forehead, representing sticking plaster, and referring to his magnificent Test innings. Television may have been in its infancy in those times but the impact made by a charismatic cricketer was still immense.

The Gentlemen–Players match in 1948 celebrated the centenary of the birth of W. G. Grace. Denis, with a brisk 43 in his second innings, helped Len Hutton orchestrate a Players' victory by seven wickets. Hutton finished the game with 132 not out, such a characteristically fine innings that the England selectors had no qualms about restoring him to their side for the next Test match. This was preceded by Middlesex *v* Australians, a fixture in which Denis batted with panache for a first innings 62 while the rest of his side struggled.

The fourth Test, at Headingley, was the one, from an England standpoint, that got away. Australia made the (then) highest winning total in the fourth innings of a Test match, 404 for three, to clinch the series, and moreover they accomplished this unprecedented performance on a wearing pitch tailor-made for spin. Alas, England left out Jack Young and entered the match with only one front-line spin bowler, Jim Laker. As it happened, Laker enjoyed no success as Australia piled up the runs on the last day. If England had accepted their chances there can be little doubt that Australia would have lost.

England had made 496 in their first innings, Washbrook making 143, Edrich 111, Hutton 81, nightwatchman Bedser 79 and Denis 23, caught behind off Lindwall when playing too fine a leg glance. Australia replied with 458, the youngest member of their side, Neil Harvey, striking a second successive Test hundred (112). When England went in again, to get 365 for eight before Yardley declared after five minutes' batting on the final morning, Hutton and Washbrook completed their second century partnership for the first wicket and Denis scored a solid 66 exactly tuned to his side's requirement. It was no time for frills or furbelows.

With so many runs at his back, Yardley still had what seemed to be an ideal setting for Denis's unorthodox left-arm spin, and lost little time in seeking to prove it. Denis soon had Lindsay Hassett caught and bowled, but he had Morris missed off a not difficult stumping chance and Bradman, who found his googly difficult to read, twice put down by Jack Crapp at slip. But the runs simply flowed on either side of the lunch interval by which time, of course, Australia could have easily lost three wickets for less than 100. Four overs of Hutton's occasional leg-breaks went for 30, and three more from Denis yielded enough runs to persuade his captain to take him off, his figures being 15–3–82–1.

I dare say that with the benefit of hindsight Yardley would have acted differently. A second new ball did nothing to slow down a second-wicket partnership which was finally ended, on 301, with Australia all but home and dry. Morris, who was missed by Laker at square leg on 126, fell to Yardley for 182. The Don finished with 173 not out.

Denis played five innings for Middlesex, with a best score of only 32, before England and Australia locked horns again at The Oval. On a saturated pitch, with further rain forecast, Yardley reluctantly opted to bat, whereupon Ray Lindwall (six for 20) bowled England out for 52, their lowest total against any country. Only Hutton, last out for 30, withstood the attack for any length of time. Denis fell to a splendid catch by Morris at backward square leg when hooking Lindwall authentically enough. He had made 4.

Few people now remember that Australia replied with a total of 389 but surely every cricketer knows that Don Bradman ended his quite unparalleled Test career with 0, bowled Eric Hollies, second ball, by a googly. Arthur Morris was run out for 196, which made him the most productive batsman on either side in the series with 696 runs at 87.00.

After that it was a case of England fighting a losing cause. Hutton resisted yet again for an admirable 64. Denis was obliged to work hard but was advancing encouragingly, on 39, when Bill Johnston had him taken one-handed by Lindwall in the gully. Bowled out for 188, England went down by an innings and 149 runs.

Denis topped the England batting averages by some distance – 562 runs at 62.44. Bedser took twice as many wickets (18) as any other England bowler although, by the subsequent standards he was soon to set, they were expensive.

After those hiccoughs in the early part of August, Denis ended his 1948 summer in the most handsome fashion. He thrashed Surrey's bowlers for 123 not out, then took a rapid 84 off those of Warwickshire. At Hastings he got a spanking 82 for the South of England against the Australians, to be followed by 135 and 125 not out, against H. D. G. Leveson-Gower's X1 at Scarborough, for the MCC team shortly to tour South Africa. The first of those hundreds was made in less than three hours, the second in just over two. In first-class matches in 1948 he scored 2,451 runs at 61.80 and took 62 wickets.

Middlesex finished third in the county championship, the title going, for the first time in their history, to Glamorgan. Remarkably enough, a key role in the Welsh triumph was played by a veteran off-spinner, J. C. Clay, then 50 years of age, who had been a member of the Glamorgan side which made its début in the championship in 1921. It goes almost without saying that the Middlesex batting averages were headed by the celebrated firm of Compton and Edrich, with Jack Robertson not far behind.

The retirement of Don Bradman at the end of an unparalleled career left Denis and Len Hutton unarguably holding centre stage. There would be good times ahead for England's cricket – provided they could produce some fast bowlers of quality and, above all, a productive partner for Alec Bedser.

1948/49: Triumph in South Africa

THE TOUR WHICH F. G. Mann's MCC side made to South Africa in 1948/49 turned out for Denis to be nothing but one long, uninterrupted triumph. Although he was outscored by Len Hutton and Cyril Washbrook in the Test series, his aggregate of runs in all first-class matches (1,781) and his eight hundreds set new records for a South African season and new targets for England batsmen abroad.

Four of those centuries were made in five innings during the early weeks of the tour, culminating in an astonishing performance at Benoni. Since Hutton's form at this time was equally resplendent, with that of Washbrook and Reg Simpson not so far behind, it is easy to see why spectators flocked in huge numbers to watch MCC briskly amass substantial totals against State opposition of a mostly modest standard. 'Wherever MCC went,' George Mann remembers, 'everyone wanted to see Len and Denis bat. They couldn't of course play in all the games, but Denis was always willing.'

MCC went unbeaten throughout the tour, just as Walter Hammond's side had done ten years earlier. They won the Test series 2–0 by gaining, at the last gasp, dramatic victories in the first and final matches of the rubber, by two and three wickets respectively. The result in each of those Tests might easily have been reversed but England, the more positive side, deserved their success.

Having begun his tour with 34 and 30 not out against Western Province, and then, greatly to local disappointment, 0 against a Country Districts X1, Denis got himself into an irresistible groove with 121 in a second fixture at Newlands, against Cape Province. He next took 150 off Griqualand West in ninety-five minutes, and 106 off a Natal attack which included a 19-year-old fast bowler, Cuan McCarthy, who took five wickets including that of the maestro, clean bowled.

But these performances were modest in the light of what was to come. Against North-Eastern Transvaal at Benoni, Denis struck the fastest triple hundred in the history of first-class cricket. His 300, out of 399, was made in one minute over three hours and he struck five sixes and forty-two fours. His first hundred came up in sixty-six minutes, the second in seventy-eight and the third in thirty-seven.

Denis played the entire innings, in stifling heat, in a long-sleeved sweater. This was to conceal a blue unguent smeared underarm to cure a nasty itch. It was so hot that one of the home side's bowlers, with nought for plenty, was taken to hospital with heart palpitations.

Who remembers the name of the batsman who was out in the middle when Denis came in? Content to play second fiddle, Reg Simpson has no regrets about being forgotten. 'I never saw anything so exhilarating,' he reports. 'When I saw the form he was in I gave him as much of the bowling as possible. In fact at one stage he came down the wicket and said, "Come on, Reg, have a knock yourself." That was typical of him. "Don't worry," I replied, "I'm enjoying it too much." ' Reg says that during his lifetime he has not seen a greater England player, and he thinks that cricket in England might have taken a different course if batsmen had not been encouraged by the run-accumulators bent on improving their averages, and by the negative coaching which brought about the dreaded pad-bat prod.

That innings, the highest of Denis's career, was in one way untypical in that, except on the sternest occasions, he was never a batsman who took fresh guard after reaching three figures to forge towards a higher score. George Mann takes credit for keeping him going at Benoni. 'The local officials asked me at one interval to tell him that he had to stay in, and the treasurer was just as keen to have him batting again on the second morning. He got the message. But murdering mediocre bowling was not his scene. He wasn't a big innings man in matches like that.'

After all this Denis descended to a more humdrum level with a mere 84 against Transvaal, whereupon the team returned to Durban for the first Test. I should add that when they had been there for the game against Natal, Denis met Valerie Platts, who was to become his second wife in 1951. The youngest of five attractive daughters of an affluent sugar planter, she had been assigned as one of the official drivers to ferry MCC around. For her introduction to Denis, Godfrey Evans stands up to be counted. 'We all had lady drivers. Valerie was allotted to Doug Wright who suggested to me that such a smasher should go to someone else. So I effected the transfer to an obvious candidate.'

At the climax of the first Test match, England were eight wickets down, with Alec Bedser and Cliff Gladwin together, 2 runs needed to win and three balls left to bowl. At that point any one of four results was possible. Off the sixth Bedser levelled the scores. Gladwin heaved at the seventh (in an eight-ball over) and missed. Another heave, and another miss, at the last, but the ball rebounded off Gladwin's thigh and a frantic leg bye brought England home. The occasion has become immortalised in cricket lore through the words of Gladwin when he went out to bat. 'Coometh the hour,' he observed, 'coometh the maan.'

South Africa's totals were 161 and 219, England's 253 and 128 for eight. Denis got 72 on a difficult turning pitch against Athol Rowan and Tufty Mann in his first innings, and a vital 28 in his second when Cuan McCarthy and co. had another testing pitch to exploit. McCarthy bowled him behind his legs as he moved a shade too much across his stumps. In the first innings Hutton fashioned an equally important 83.

Accompanied by E. W. Swanton and Denis, George Mann set off by road for Johannesburg and the second Test match. Jim Swanton tells the tale of a breakdown miles from anywhere and of how, while waiting for someone to pass by, they got out their golf clubs for some chipping practice. In due time an Afrikaans family appeared. 'We'll send yew help from the next garage,' they assured them. But half an hour later the same car turned up again. 'Aren't yew Denis Compton?' the driver enquired, 'I realised I hadn't got your autograph.'

In the next Test match, played for the first time at the Ellis Park Stadium in Johannesburg, Hutton (158), Washbrook (195) and Compton (114) were principal contributors to a massive England total of 608, the two opening batsmen setting a then world record Test partnership of 359 for the first wicket. Washbrook remembers the pitch as being the most perfect he ever encountered, and Denis's stroke play and improvisation as a joy to behold.

South Africa were bowled out for 315, followed on and finished at 270 for two when the game ended, predictably in a draw. Eric Rowan got 156 not out in South Africa's second innings, wearing plimsolls, I understand, and no gloves or box. His form in his previous Test innings had been unconvincing. On account of long-distance travel problems the Springbok selectors announced their side for the third Test before Rowan went in again for the second innings. He was dropped from the third Test side, but was duly recalled for the fourth.

The third Test, played in Cape Town at the New Year, was also drawn although Mann, dangling the carrot in hope of a positive result, declared England's second innings to set South Africa a target of 229 in two hours and five minutes. The home side settled quietly for a final score of 142 for four.

It might have been a good toss for Dudley Nourse to lose since England in their first innings found themselves having to cope with a lively, greenish pitch and later in the innings with Athol Rowan who found some appreciable turn. Dragging a ball on to his wicket, Denis was bowled by Rowan for 1, but after England had done well to make 308, he took five wickets for 70, in his old orthodox style, as South Africa gained a lead of 48. Bruce Mitchell and Dudley Nourse got hundreds, both of them falling to Denis, the captain to an excellent return catch. In England's second innings, 276 for three declared, Hutton scored 87 and Denis was 51 not out at the closure.

It seemed inevitable that sooner or later Denis had to descend from dizzy peaks. Having scored his sixth hundred of the tour, against Eastern Province, he made 4 in his one innings in the Transvaal game, 60 (on a difficult pitch) and 25 not out against Rhodesia in Bulawayo, and 34 in a second encounter with them in Salisbury. Next, in the fourth Test back in Johannesburg, he managed a modest 24 and 25.

This encounter resulted in a third successive draw, South Africa being set, after another declaration by England, the tall order of making 376 in four and a half hours. They declined the bait, Eric Rowan signalling his return to form by batting through for 86 not out in a final total of 194 for four. Washbrook got 97 and Watkins 111 in England's first innings of 379, and Hutton scored a commanding 123 in their second one. For South Africa there was another hundred by Nourse and some more fine off-spin bowling from Athol Rowan.

The next fixture, against a Natal X1 at Pietermaritzburg, saw Denis return to his exuberant best. A declaration by Nourse, which set MCC 270 to make in the last innings in just over two hours, was just the sort of challenge he enjoyed. His 141, made in ninety-nine minutes, included one six and twenty fours. MCC, four wickets down, were only 10 short at the finish.

So to the fifth Test match in Port Elizabeth, where South Africa, to square the series, had to take a positive stance. There was little in it on first innings: South Africa 379 with 99 from Mitchell in his last Test and 125 from their wicket keeper, Billy Wade; England 395 with a rousing and critical 136 not out by their captain. Denis got 49, caught behind off Tufty Mann.

Now it was up to Nourse, whose declaration left England with 172 to make in ninety-five minutes. They went at it from the start, with Denis contributing a frisky 42 before he fell to Athol Rowan. At the climax – almost as frenzied as it had been in the first Test – there was one minute of playing time left when Jack Crapp hit 10 runs from three consecutive balls to give England their second victory in the rubber by three wickets.

Having concluded his Test series with an aggregate of 406 runs at

50.75, Denis still had time to make another stirring hundred, in the last fixture of the tour, against Combined Universities in Cape Town. He signed off with 125 made in two and a quarter hours, as well as six wickets for 62. As I have mentioned earlier, Denis took 24 catches on the tour, apparently without dropping a thing.

His first tour of South Africa has been recalled by Denis as one of the happiest periods in his cricketing life. He has written that George Mann, who combined strength with great charm, was the most effective captain he played under, and the side the happiest he ever toured with. 'Of all the countries I have played cricket against I have always liked South Africa, and the South Africans, best.' From that early loyalty and admiration he has never swerved.

An interesting footnote to this tour was supplied by Gerald Brodribb when he provided some statistics for E. W. Swanton's sketch of Denis's career to that point. It was estimated that for most of his innings over 50 up to and including the tour of South Africa he scored his runs at an average of about 47 an hour. This was 12 above the general average and roughly equal to that of Bradman over his whole career.

1949: More Highs Than Lows

Iɴ 1949, when we enjoyed one of our rare good summers, Denis scored nine more hundreds – two of them against New Zealand in a four-match Test series – celebrated his benefit with what was comfortably a record return for a Middlesex player and helped his county share the championship with Yorkshire. Yet compared with previous standards his form was rather unpredictable. It was a season of highs and lows.

Two highlights occurred in May when after a sedate beginning, he made 140 in two hours and forty minutes against Northants, and 179 in an hour longer against Lancashire. It is also worth noting that he got 63 for MCC in their game with the New Zealanders in front of a first-day crowd of 28,000. How times have changed. In these days, when Cornhill Test matches and limited-overs games draw the biggest crowds, even a Graeme Hick must play most of his cricket in front of a modest-sized audience.

At his benefit match, Middlesex v Sussex over the Whitsun holiday, 55,000 spectators were present during the three days, and Denis certainly ensured that Monday's crowd got their money's worth. It was wholly characteristic of him that an occasion such as this should have inspired him to play one of his very finest innings. *Wisden* records that he adjusted himself to the pace of the pitch with considerable care, but the last 79 runs in his 182 were made in forty-five minutes with a magnificent exhibition of driving.

The first Test, at Headingley, was now all but due, and it was already clear that a New Zealand side led by the wise and dignified Walter Hadlee (father of Richard) was not short of batting strength. They had two great left-handers, Bert Sutcliffe and Martin Donnelly, each of whom was to finish his tour with well over 2,000 runs. They also had a very good right-hand batsman, Mervyn Wallace, who at one time looked well on the way towards a thousand before the end of May, although his form then declined.

In that era Australia and South Africa were the only countries to play Test matches in England scheduled to last for four days. Those of 1949 were limited to three days and consequently the outcome of the series, on good pitches in memorably pleasant weather, was disappointing; all four Tests were drawn. Denis remembers it as the most boring series he ever played in. He felt that, whatever else happened, New

Zealand had no intention of losing. This, I think, was an uncharitable judgement, although it is true that Hadlee's side played the entire series with just four front-line bowlers.

At Headingley, some restrictive New Zealand outcricket certainly made England work hard for their first innings 372. It took Len Hutton more than four hours to make 101, and Denis almost as long to score 114. New Zealand replied with 341, Trevor Bailey marking his Test debut with six for 118. Cyril Washbrook was 103 not out when England declared their second innings at 267 for four (Denis having made 26), and proceedings ended quietly with New Zealand on 195 for two.

Back with Middlesex, Denis had two failures against Yorkshire (which will not have pleased him) at Lord's and one against Gloucestershire in Bristol. Tom Graveney, who got 96 in that match, saw Denis play for the first time, although he had seen him on film. He didn't see much now. Denis was 'c Milton b Goddard 0' – one of the rare occasions when a wily old bird had Denis's wicket cheaply.

Denis was back in the runs in the second Test, at Lord's, making 116 and sharing a sixth wicket stand of 189 with Bailey during the early stages of which he found himself outscored by a partner positively frolicsome in his approach. England's declaration at 313 for nine on the first evening held interest in that it was illegal. At that time an experimental law permitting such an event on the first day of a three-day match did not apply to this particular Test series. England's captain, George Mann, duly made an honourable apology. The closure had led to no English advantage.

Martin Donnelly's 206, which completed a notable Lord's hat-trick for him (he had made hundreds for Oxford in the University match and for Gentlemen v Players), virtually ensured another draw. New Zealand scored 484, whereupon England played out the match by making 306 for five. Jack Robertson, replacing an injured Washbrook, scored 121 but was never again selected for a Test match in England. Washbrook was restored to England's side for the next Test, during which Jack made 331 not out, the highest score ever made by a Middlesex player, *in one day* at Worcester.

By then, Denis had remained on song in doing his stuff for Paddy Corrall's benefit at Leicester; he was run out for 99 made in even time. This was followed by 122 at Bramall Lane, his first hundred against Yorkshire. It took him almost five hours, but still gave him much satisfaction. Brian Close, who was in his first season for Yorkshire, recalls what a thrill it was to get an occasional ball past the great man's bat. 'In those days the best batters didn't miss much. Nowadays they play and miss twice an over. No wonder wicket keepers stay fit.'

For the third Test match, at Old Trafford, Freddie Brown took over the England captaincy to play his first Test match for twelve years, and Brian Close, at the age of 18 and 149 days, became the youngest cricketer to make his England debut. Brown did the positive thing by putting his opponents in to bat. New Zealand made 293 (Bailey six for 84) but by the time England had replied with 440 for nine declared, another match was destined to be drawn. Reg Simpson got 103, Bailey 72 not out and Denis was bowled by Jack Cowie for 25. Donnelly had scores of 75 and 80. Sutcliffe got 101 in New Zealand's second innings of 348 for seven, at which point the match ended in a draw.

Before the teams met again Denis scored 102 not out against Hampshire and took 80s off both Kent and Surrey. But there were some low scores, too, and he made 13 when the fourth Test match at The Oval proved to be just as inconclusive as the previous three. The only difference was that one side, England, thought they could sniff success when New Zealand batted in the third and last innings of the game. A combative young all-rounder, John Reid, then 21 years of age, put paid to such optimism with a rugged 93.

This was the Test match when Denis made a well-chronicled late arrival on the last morning. Held up at the lights just short of Vauxhall Bridge, the time being 11.05 a.m., he heard a friendly taxi driver suggest that he ought to put his foot down. 'I'm OK thanks,' Denis said, 'I'll be there.' The taxi driver then invited him to listen to radio commentary on play which of course had been scheduled to start half an hour earlier.

The Oval Test match was made memorable by Len Hutton's 206, his second hundred coming with a blaze of graceful strokes in only eight-five minutes. England, who had packed their side with bowlers in an attempt to get a positive result, scored 482 for a first innings lead of 137. New Zealand subsequently declared at 308 for nine, and that was that. Their claim to four-day Test matches could be resisted no longer.

Sutcliffe and Donnelly finished that series with aggregates exceeded only by Hutton (469). Denis had a tally of exactly 300 at 50.00 and the pleasure of heading the bowling averages, with five wickets. Trevor Bailey certainly made a strong initial impact with sixteen wickets and a batting average in the 70s.

Denis still had time that season to take a third hundred, 148, off the New Zealanders' bowling, in their game against Middlesex, and to get another, 127, for MCC against Yorkshire at Scarborough. He also got

97 not out when Middlesex, in their last championship fixture, had to beat Derbyshire at Lord's in order to be sure of sharing the title.

Needing 193 in the last innings, Middlesex collapsed to 36 for five against the lively bowling of the well-known Derbyshire trio of Copson, Gladwin and Jackson. Before he went out to join Denis, who remained in total control at one end, Walter Robins was asked what his and the remaining batsmen's approach should be. Let J. J. Warr now pick up the story. 'Play for Denis of course, the skipper says, whereupon he hits his first ball for six and adds 90 with Compo in seventy minutes. Eventually he gets out, and so does big Les (Denis's older brother). I have a nasty vision of walking out at number 11, in my first season, to settle the championship. Then Jim Sims goes in at number 9 and he says "Don't worry, I'll play for Denny's hundred." We're all expecting the forward block when he has two awful slogs for four, and the match is won.'

Earlier in this contest Cliff Gladwin was much aggrieved to have been run out by his partner. His return to base was shortly followed by a shattering of glass. 'The equanimity of the Lord's pavilion,' *Wisden* has recorded with due tact, 'was disturbed when Gladwin . . . accidentally put his bat through the dressing-room window.' In due course Gladwin was summoned to explain this curious incident to MCC's secretary, Col Rait-Kerr. 'I threw it on the floor,' the culprit explained, 'and it bounced off the 'andle like a pogo stick.'

Denis ended his summer with a return of 2,530 runs at 48.65, not to mention 73 wickets. But he was overshadowed by Hutton who enjoyed his finest home season with an aggregate of 3,429, a record 1,294 of them being made in June and another 1,050 in August.

His benefit season brought Denis £12,200 which was comfortably a Middlesex record exceeded only, in national terms, by Cyril Washbrook's £14,000 in Lancashire the previous year. It was disappointing none the less; the Middlesex committee had set themselves a target of at least £15,000. Peter Parfitt alleges that some of the late monies that accrued to the Middlesex beneficiary were banked with Barclays at their St John's Wood branch. For five years the manager wrote to Denis advising him that he was more than £1,000 in credit, and what would he like him to do? 'Eventually he nails him at Lord's and a cheque book is later issued. Within a week the account was overdrawn.'

It was also a season in which a young boy at Tonbridge School, Colin Cowdrey, was summoned from class to play with Denis in one of his benefit games, at Horsmonden in the Kentish Weald. 'What a thrill,' he remembers. 'We had a partnership of about 120 and although I got very few I did manage to play one rather good cover drive. Walking off later, Compo said, "One day you must teach me that shot." In the last over before lunch a 14-year-old off-spinner was put on. Compo took pains to hit the first five balls to different fielders and then deliberately but not too obviously missed the last one, outside the off stump. He then ruffled the young man's hair on his way back to the pavilion and said, "Very well bowled." ' Soon afterwards, Denis reported back to Highbury for his last football season.

1950: Difficult Days

A T THE END OF APRIL 1950 Denis bowed out of football after Arsenal had won the FA Cup at Wembley. The cricket season which followed is a significant one in this story since it marked the time when his knee broke down altogether at the end of May. His future career as a cricketer was now at risk and he was advised to have an immediate operation in the London Clinic. Even the most optimistic prognosis indicated that he would have to live with a restriction of movement in the knee. The operation was as successful as could be expected and he was back in the middle again by the end of July. But it is easy to understand why it took him the best part of a year to adjust himself mentally to the truth. It was as if a finely tuned engine had been reduced by a governor to about seventy per cent of its capacity.

The knee gave him pain throughout the first month of the season yet he did well enough. He contrived to make 144 for Middlesex against Somerset at Lord's, followed by 75 when Glamorgan came to town. The crisis finally arrived during the Whitsun match against Sussex. A brave innings of 50 left him in dire straits on the first evening and he was admitted to the London Clinic next day.

Shortly afterwards, the national selectors staged a Test trial, England v The Rest, at Bradford, where Jim Laker did them, as well as the Rest batsmen, no favours by returning the startling bowling analysis of eight wickets for 2 runs. 'And one of those,' he would always tell you afterwards, 'was a single to Eric Bedser to get him off the mark.'

At this juncture no one, least of all Denis himself, knew whether he would be able to play any sort of part in a four-match Test series against the West Indies. The potential of the touring side could not be under-rated by anyone who had seen their impressive 2–0 victory in a home series against an admittedly inadequate England team in 1947/48.

The famous triumvirate – Everton Weekes, Frank Worrell and Clyde Walcott – was already putting county attacks to the sword and there was sure evidence that the West Indians had two young spin bowlers of considerable talent. One of them, Alfred Valentine, was a slow left-hander who gave the ball a real tweak. The other was Sonny Ramadhin the direction of whose spin, after a quick flurry of an action, was distinctly hard to detect.

As it happened, neither of them played an especially notable role in the first Test at Old Trafford in which Norman Yardley won a handy toss for England and the West Indies had little chance in the fourth innings on a crumbling pitch. England, who included *three* spinners – Eric Hollies, Laker and Bob Berry – won by 202 runs.

How very different the story at Lord's where the West Indies and their supporters rejoiced over their first win in England in what is now enshrined in cricket lore as the 'Calypso Test'. Enmeshed in the spinners' web, England were bowled out for 151 and 274 and lost by 326 runs. Ramadhin had eleven wickets all told for 152 runs off 115 overs, Valentine seven for 127 off 116. Such figures speak for themselves. Cyril Washbrook battled away to make 114 in England's second innings.

Walcott had struck a powerful 168 not out when John Goddard declared the second West Indian innings closed at 425 for six. Denis thought Walcott, whose Test record in the Caribbean was immense, the best of the three Ws.

By the time the third Test took place at Trent Bridge Denis was well on his way to a recovery, a good deal more encouraging than the gloomier forecasts had indicated. He worked his way back into something still short of full working order by playing several out-matches for MCC in the second half of July.

There was no respite for England in Nottingham where Len Hutton had to pull out with an attack of lumbago and Harold Gimblett of Somerset declared that a boil on his neck would prevent him taking Hutton's place. It would have been Gimblett's first Test match since 1939. He was not selected by England again.

England's first innings on a bland pitch, 223, was simply not enough. West Indies rattled up a total of 558, Frank Worrell contributing a silken 261 and Everton Weekes a trenchant 129. Washbrook got another hundred, 102, and Simpson 94 in England's second innings of 436, but it was not good enough. West Indies took a 2–1 lead in the series with victory by ten wickets. Four days later, Denis, to general delight, returned to the first-class scene in the most encouraging fashion.

The occasion was Laurie Fishlock's benefit match, Surrey *v* Middlesex, at The Oval where over the three days not far short of 50,000 spectators gathered to honour the beneficiary and to welcome back a national hero. He marked it with what in the circumstances can surely be described as a triumphant hundred – 115 not out skilfully but not recklessly composed in three and three-quarter hours. To this, his 85th century, he added 25 in the second innings. The old footwork seemed in goodish order, but getting off the mark for a quick single posed problems. This may have explained how Don Bennett, then making his initial appearance for Middlesex as a 16-year-old, was run out. 'It was the only time I ever got run out when partnering Denis,' he recalls with refreshing honesty, 'and it wasn't his fault.'

Denis's performance against Surrey was closely monitored by national selectors anxious to be reassured that his name could be one of the twelve then announced as being certain starters for the forthcoming tour of Australia. He had made 68 and 28 in his next game, against Leicestershire, when he was chosen to play in the fourth and last Test of the summer. But, first, he had a further county fixture, at Hove.

On the second (Monday) morning of the Sussex game there was no sign of Denis when Middlesex took the field. Eventually, there was a screech of brakes in the car park at about 12.50 p.m. followed by a much overdue appearance on the field – in plimsolls. 'He had the usual problems with his gear,' John Warr relates. 'Robby (the captain R. W. V. Robins) asked him where the hell he'd been and, to get his own back, promptly put him on to bowl. With the customary golden touch Compo, no trouble at all, acquired two quick wickets. That didn't please one member of Sussex who subsequently accused Robby of cheating, by holding Compo back. The skipper wasn't best pleased. He got big Les to help frogmarch the member into the Sussex committee room where an apology was demanded.' Denis got 80 in his second innings by way of atonement.

All thoughts of England squaring the Test series at The Oval were abandoned some while before West Indies completed a first innings of 503. Frank Worrell got 138 and the left-handed Allan Rae, whose solid qualities blended effectively with the elegant ones of Jeffrey Stollmeyer, scored 109.

An unblemished 202 not out from Len Hutton, who carried his bat through their innings, could not save England from following on. Denis had made 44 in a stand of 109 with Hutton and all seemed set fair when he set off for what looked a comfortable single to his partner in the direction of fine leg. Hutton sent him back but Denis by then had passed the point of no return.

Having been bowled out in their first innings for 344, England succumbed to Valentine (six wickets) and Ramadhin (three) for 103, to lose by an innings and 56 runs. In his second effort Denis was caught off Valentine for 11. But it was Ramadhin who set him greater problems. He has admitted that he found it difficult to read the little man's spin, although it was to be a different matter in the clearer light of the

Caribbean when they met again. Denis has said that Hutton, even after that double hundred, could not be sure of unravelling the mysteries either.

Denis finished this season on a low note but had the pleasure of captaining his county for the first time, in their home match against Northants. It is worth recording that Middlesex had no fewer than seven captains at one time or another in 1950, the others being Robins, Edrich, Dewes, Jim Sims, Gubby Allen and George Mann. This must have contributed in part to their decline in the championship from equal first to fourteenth place. The loss of Bill Edrich for five weeks during the period of Denis's recuperation was of course an added blow. But new blood was needed. The newly elected Cambridge captain, J. J. Warr, would be regularly available after 1951 to stiffen bowling which had been carried this summer by Jack Young. A 17-year-old off-spinner, Fred Titmus, made promising progress.

Denis averaged 56.78 in the championship, and overall in first-class matches scored 957 runs at 45.57. So he failed, for the first time in his career, and for a good reason, to pass the thousand mark. I might add that during the four-match Test rubber, in which England suffered some frustrating injuries, their selectors chose twenty-five players. The West Indies, as they were to do in 1988, made do with twelve. So it is not just in the latest era that England's selectors have chopped and changed. Selection, and captaincy, are much easier assignments when a side is winning.

The season of 1950, as I have indicated earlier, marked the start of the third phase in Denis's career during which he had to live from day to day with that fractious knee. It is remarkable, in spite of such a handicap, what he still managed to achieve.

1950/51: Test Failure in Australia

In SEPTEMBER 1950 an MCC side led by Freddie Brown sailed off to Fremantle not only in quest of the Ashes, which had not been in England's keeping since 1934, but of their first Test victory over Australia since the war. Brown, whose leadership turned out to be a hugely popular success, was appointed after Norman Yardley and George Mann declared themselves unable to tour. The even-time hundred Brown had made in the 1950 Gentlemen – Players match must have been an opportune reminder of pugnacious powers undimmed at the age of 40. Denis was named as vice-captain – the first professional to be so honoured.

The subsequent failures of young players such as David Sheppard, John Dewes, Gilbert Parkhouse and Brian Close – then only a raw 19-year-old – served to underline the surprising omission of seasoned batsmen such as Bill Edrich, Jack Robertson, Dennis Brookes and Harold Gimblett.

But no one's failure in the Test series was more dramatic than that of Denis Compton who began it, as E. W. Swanton has observed in *Elusive Victory*, with a Test average second only amongst Englishmen to that of Herbert Sutcliffe and more Test centuries than any other Englishman except Jack Hobbs and Walter Hammond.

England's elusive victory was achieved at long last in the final Test in Melbourne, but not before Australia had won the first four matches in the rubber. Denis had to miss the second one on account of injury but he knows, as his colleagues know, that another 20 or 30 from him at crucial moments could well have tilted the series the other way. To be fair, the same must apply in the case of Cyril Washbrook, who also had a thin time. 'We were the better side in three Tests,' Denis has said, 'yet we only won the fifth.'

Denis's knee gave an ominous sign when it swelled up again shortly before the team left England. X-rays revealed no discernible floating bone chips and his surgeons advised him that he would have to live with the problems. There was some improvement on the voyage out, but it was playing up again when he struggled to get 7 in the first of two up-country games in Western Australia. In the second of these he made 76, with a good deal less discomfort, and that set him going. A hundred (106) against Western Australia was followed by another (107) in the State game with Victoria in which he became the first professional cricketer to captain an England side abroad since Arthur Shrewsbury in 1887. The climate of opinion was changing: within eighteen months Len Hutton became the first professional to captain England.

The Melbourne fixture gave them their first taste of Jack Iverson, a 'freak' bowler whose stock ball, a googly, was flicked off the third finger from the front of his hand. He attacked the leg stump, using his height (6ft 2in) to extract extra bounce, and Denis, then with his knee problems, has attested that he was always difficult to get away. He found it risky to sweep the googly. In this first encounter Denis was reported by Jim Swanton to have made a frenetic start. He should have been stumped almost at once but later settled into 'a saner groove'.

Denis next had the doubtful pleasure of leading MCC while New South Wales ran up a total of 509 for three wickets in Sydney, Keith Miller scoring a regal 214 and Arthur Morris a sumptuous 168. 'I was persuaded by Walter Robins,' Freddie Brown remembers, 'that Denis was a very good skipper with lots of imagination.' Needing all his resourcefulness as the ball whistled past him with great regularity, Denis sought Len Hutton's advice. 'I fancy,' Len wryly observed, 'that you'd better send for some more bowlers.' Bedser was feeling the after-effects of 'flu and Doug Wright was frustrated by a painful back.

There was no decline in Denis's batting form when he scored 92 and 34 not out in this drawn game, but it was a different story when the tourists played Queensland in Brisbane before the start of the Test series. His 28 was described in *Elusive Victory* as being utterly out of character.

England took a big chance on Wright's fitness but left out John Warr, who had done well against Queensland but whose fielding was held to be a liability. So they went into the rubber with only four bowlers. They brought in the reserve wicket keeper, Arthur McIntyre, and decided to have Hutton stiffen the middle order at number 5. The opening batsmen were Reg Simpson and Cyril Washbrook, whose form after a late arrival had thus far been second only to that of Denis himself.

Local opinion held firmly that Australia, even without Don Bradman but otherwise still with substantially the same old side, would win the series easily. 'England's stock,' Jack Fingleton wrote, 'has never been so low here on the eve of the first Test.' Sadly, Jack had crossed his great divide before Mike Gatting's team arrived in Brisbane, another apparent nadir reached, in 1986/87. The remarkable win pulled off by

Gatting's men on that occasion might so well have been mirrored in 1950.

Against all the odds, and after an important toss had been lost, England, by some inspired outcricket, with Godfrey Evans in spectacular fettle behind the stumps, bowled out Australia on a good pitch for 228. But later that first evening the heavens opened and England knew they faced the music when play was resumed on the third day. In the half hour available before lunch Simpson and Washbrook batted with aplomb and courage to make 28 together. Then, in the next four hours, twenty wickets went down for 102 runs.

Denis thought the pitch was not quite so impossibly spiteful as it had been in the corresponding Test match four years earlier, but it was nevertheless bad enough. By mid-afternoon, after Freddie Brown had declared so that his bowlers might have another crack at Australia while the pitch retained its vice, England lost seven wickets for 68. Denis, 3, was given out caught by Lindwall after aiming a hook against a ball from Johnston that got up higher than he expected and brushed his forearm some inches above the wrist. The umpire was later honest enough to admit that he had made a mistake.

Australia in their second innings fared even worse than England had, losing seven wickets to Bailey and Bedser for 32 before Lindsay Hassett declared in his turn to leave England, their final target 193, with seventy minutes to bat at the end of a dramatic day.

They held out for an hour, while losing the wickets of Simpson, Washbrook and Dewes, but the last ten minutes were disastrous. Bailey, uncharacteristically enough, was caught when hooking a long hop, Bedser was taken at cover off a dismal stroke and, worse still in the circumstances, McIntyre was run out when attempting one too many. That left Evans and Hutton together, and England on 30 for six. Denis had been held back for the morrow. But alas on the fourth morning, after Evans had been caught at short leg off Johnston, Denis pushed the first ball he received from that bowler into the same fielder's hands.

There was no hope for England after that, although Len Hutton, on a pitch now easier but not unblemished, blazed away with some marvellous shots in a final act of defiance. England were all out for 122, losing by 70 runs. Hutton's innings (62 not out) is still remembered with awe by those who saw it.

It is easy to see that Denis's failure on that last morning virtually sealed England's fate. It did nothing to lift his morale or confidence and, at about this time, too, the news was released of a divorce from his first wife, Doris, whom he had married in 1941. Yet within a few days he was back in the old groove with 92 made in just fifty minutes against a Queensland Country team. The last thing he wanted now was a recurrence of a familiar problem, but the knee flared up once more when he was fielding against an Australian XI in Sydney. It took him four painful hours to make another hundred (115). When MCC followed on, it seemed highly imprudent, with the second Test now imminent, to let him bat again. But in he went, without a runner, to make 29 when the game was comfortably saved.

The knee was now so inflamed and swollen that, although the tour selection committee was not of one mind, Denis eventually had to say that he could not risk himself playing in the Melbourne Test. Freddie Brown reluctantly agreed that this was the right decision and England, without one of their great batsmen, were now to lose another match they might so easily have won.

On this occasion the skipper was not greatly upset to lose the toss, as Bedser contributed a magnificent piece of bowling on a green pitch when Australia batted first. At times he was virtually unplayable. The English players lost count of how many times the batsmen, notably Neil Harvey, played and missed. Bailey, scarcely less effective, shared eight wickets with him as Australia made 194. To this, in easier conditions, England disappointingly replied with only 197. It would have been much less but for some stern defence from Bailey, a belligerent 62 from Brown and a very useful 49 from Evans.

The captain followed this staunch effort by bowling at medium pace and capturing four cheap wickets in an Australian second innings of 181. All of his bowlers had done their job. Now it was up to the batsmen to do theirs as they sought to score 179, which would have been the lowest total of the match. But they failed by 28 runs. Hutton, once more at no.5, got top score, 40. Christmas sunshine had helped to widen some cracks on the pitch, and the odd ball kept low. Denis thought the decision to get the runs the hard way was misguided. 'We could have done it if we'd thrown off the shackles and shown more nerve.'

It was after this Test match, when larking about at a private late evening party, that Denis fell on to a standpipe in his host's garden. Stitches had to be inserted to a wound about a blackened right eye. Next morning, he was not on the team's plane bound for Sydney. 'Where is Compton?' the media enquired. 'He's coming later,' was all the captain said. But of course the story broke – with its inevitable innuendoes. Keith Miller, it appears, had contrived to get a picture taken by a photographer on his Sydney newspaper. It looked awful. Denis, who had been quite sober when the incident occurred, felt ill-used. I believe it was the one time his relationship with an old Australian buddy was under strain.

Having missed the return game with New South Wales in which Hutton made 150 and Simpson 259, Denis returned to the England side for the third Test, also in Sydney. Their luck was not yet due for turning. In the first innings of the match, Bailey had his thumb fractured by Lindwall, and Wright tore a groin muscle. England were reduced to three front-line bowlers, Bedser, Warr and Brown, all of whom did well to hold Australia to a total of 426. But Australia took a lead of 136, and Iverson then took six wickets for 27 as England were shot out for 123. Australia's victory by an innings and 13 runs gave them certain victory in the series and a renewed lease on the Ashes.

Denis got another Test nought in his first innings, dragging the third ball he received on to his stumps. In a magnificent spell Miller took the wickets of Hutton, Compton and Simpson for 5 runs. He had also taken a blinding catch at slip to dismiss Washbrook, and in Australia's only innings made 145 not out.

Denis has confessed that he never felt so tense as when he went out to bat in the second innings. Having taken fifteen minutes to avoid a pair, he battled away for the best part of two hours to reach 23. He then got a bottom edge to a ball from Johnston that was diverted off the instep of Tallon, the wicket keeper, up to Ian Johnson at slip. There are some strange ways of getting out in this game of cricket, never more so perhaps than when a man is struggling.

Denis had now made 26 in four Test innings, but in other matches the runs continued to flow. Against Tasmania in Hobart he got 44 and 77 not out, completing MCC's victory with six consecutive fours. The day before that match, in which Denis was captain, Brian Close reported back to the hotel with a note from a doctor saying he ought not to play for a month because of a groin injury. 'Denis took one look at it,' Close reports, 'tore it up and said, "I don't care what the bloody medico says. You're playing!" '

Against a Combined XI in Hobart Denis went faster to make 142 in only two hours and ten minutes. Surely, with form such as this, his impact on the Test rubber could not be very long delayed?

It was not to be. Australia (371 and 403 for eight declared) defeated England (272 and 228) in the fourth Test in Adelaide by the conclusive margin of 274 runs. Denis was out for 5 in his first innings, caught behind down the leg side off Lindwall, and then for 0, second ball, when he nudged a catch off Johnston to short leg, a reprise of his earlier dismissal in the Brisbane Test.

This was the Test in which Len Hutton once again batted throughout an England innings for a masterly 165 not out, and Freddie Brown, driving home with the manager, Brigadier Green, from a state dinner, met an immovable object in the shape of an Adelaide lamp standard. The manager had his nose broken. The captain had enough cuts and bruises to stop him from adding to the three overs he had bowled in the second innings.

In the final Test, in Melbourne, Bedser and Brown, sharing all ten wickets, gave England's batsmen a splendid opportunity to take control. (This after Bailey had turned an ankle and in spite of the captain's painful shoulder.) In one spell Brown disposed of Morris, Harvey and Miller without conceding a run. Denis held a stunning slip catch off Bedser's bowling to dismiss Lindwall.

At one point, in reply to Australia's 217, England stood at 171 for one, but Lindwall and Miller tore out the heart of the innings and Denis was one of their victims. Lindwall looked close to the end of a new-ball spell, and Denis had seemingly discovered the old touch, when Lindwall had him caught at second slip for 11. Reg Simpson, batting at number 3, made an exciting 156 not out, his finest Test innings, but no one stayed with him long and England had to settle for 320.

A handy lead of 103 was made to look much better when Bedser, with another five wickets, played the leading role as Australia were bowled out again, this time for 197. England thus needed only 95 and at last a victory seemed firmly in their sights. Denis (11 not out) was in at the finish – as he was later to be when the Ashes were regained in 1953 – but it was appropriate that the winning hit should be made by Len Hutton, the outstanding batsman on either side. England won by eight wickets to end an Australian run of twenty-five Test matches without defeat. There could be no argument about it: they had lost the toss on a good pitch.

With 79 and 60 not out Hutton brought his series aggregate to 533 runs at an average of 88.83. With 30 wickets at 16.05 Bedser proved himself a giant. But what of Denis, with Test scores of 3, 0, 0, 23, 5, 0, 11 and 11 not out?

None of the greatest batsmen, I believe, has endured so bad a Test sequence as this. In 1902, in three Tests against Australia, C. B. Fry scored 0, 0, 1 and 4. In the same series – also in three matches – K. S.

Ranjitsinhji managed 13, 0, 2 and 4. In three successive Tests against England in 1907/08 the great Australian, Victor Trumper, got 4, 0, 0, 0 and 10, but then put matters right with 166. Peter May, as reported on a later page, had a very lean time in the Test matches played in South Africa in 1956/57.

Denis admitted that he reached a level of depression unequalled throughout his career, but declined to use his knee injury as an excuse. Long days in the field on hard Australian grounds imposed extra strain. Had he played only when the knee seemed in reasonable shape he might have appeared in no more than half a dozen games.

His reaction to adversity has drawn some glowing tributes from fellow players. Freddie Brown, who still doesn't quite know how he failed in the Tests, says that no one was more loyal. Len Hutton affirms that Denis had so much bad luck, it was amazing that he remained outwardly so cheerful. 'He never complained. He accepted decisions with calmness and dignity. His guts and courage were things to admire.' Echoing these sentiments, Trevor Bailey says he remained, as always, a great tourist. Even the Australians felt sorry for him, a tribute indeed.

Reg Simpson admits even now that the run of low scores was impossible to understand. 'I think,' he says, 'that by the time he had missed the second Test his confidence had tumbled. He knew how much we depended on him and as a result he obviously "tensed up" and became too set on defence. The Aussies then crowded him in the field and after that he always seemed to get out before he'd had time to settle in and relax.'

On the final leg of that tour Denis got 78 against Auckland and then, in the first, drawn Test against New Zealand, a 79, the first time he had got past 50 in a Test match since 1949. In the second, won by England by six wickets, he scored 10 and 18. He was thankful to get home again. Better things, much better things, were round the corner.

1951: All But 1,000 in May

FOR THE HOME SEASON OF 1951 Denis had already been appointed joint captain of Middlesex with Bill Edrich. It seemed that when Walter Robins called it a day the county committee made a needless and, as it turned out, unsatisfactory compromise. Denis thought it prudent to apply himself at early season net practice with unaccustomed enthusiasm.

On May 21, sixteen days after beginning the serious business, he had made 673 runs in six innings and, with the chance of seven more to come that month, looked well in line to get a thousand before the end of May.

He began with 113 against Leicestershire at Lord's, he and Edrich (who should have been with him on the recent tour) putting on 181 for the second wicket. Against Oxford University in the Parks he gave the undergraduates a good taste of his quality with 158 in just over three hours, with two sixes and twenty-nine fours, and 15 not out. Returning to Lord's, he struck a dazzling 169 in Jack Robertson's benefit match, the Whitsun fixture with Sussex, followed by 66 not out against Worcestershire and 147 for MCC against the touring South Africans. To the Springbok players who had suffered at his hands in 1947 it must have seemed that nothing had changed.

Bad weather denied him the opportunity to bat again in that game. He then came down from a dizzy pedestal with 5 and 5 against Hampshire, 11 and 15 against Lancashire. Thus, when Warwickshire came to Lord's, and lost the toss, Denis needed another 291, a very tall order indeed. He responded with a fifth hundred, the biggest yet, 172. That left him requiring 119 in the second innings on May 30. He was lbw to Eric Hollies for 33. His aggregate for that merry month was 909.

There could be not the slightest doubt about his form or confidence. The knee was holding up well. But he still needed to reassure himself that he had not lost his touch in Test matches. His 112 in the first match of a new series promptly laid any such fears to rest.

After their defeat in England in 1947 South Africa had lost the 1949/50 home series, 4–0, to Australia. Their prospects in 1951 were not enhanced when the captain, Dudley Nourse, fractured his left thumb in the Gloucestershire fixture at Bristol, only three weeks before the start of the first Test. In spite of that, Nourse played at Trent Bridge, made a courageous 208 and led his country to their first Test win in sixteen years.

Nourse held the South African piece together as they reached 483 for nine before he declared, whereupon Reg Simpson made the first Test hundred (137) by a Nottinghamshire player at Trent Bridge and Denis completed his fourth successive Test century on that ground. He was out, caught behind, when projecting a hook at McCarthy, whose suspect action generated exceptional pace. England were nine wickets down when their forthright captain, Freddie Brown, declared 64 runs behind.

A thunderstorm on the Sunday meant that batting thereafter was no joy. Denis had needed more than five hours to get his runs, and Bedser, now finding a pitch to his liking, took six wickets for 37 as South Africa were bowled out a second time for 121. That left England to get 186 in the last innings, but the South African spinners, Athol Rowan and Tufty Mann, had them out for 114. Denis fell lbw to one of Rowan's off-breaks for 5.

This was a good game of cricket but a disappointing result for England after the tonic wine of their success in Melbourne not long before. They proceeded to put things right by winning the next two Test matches, drawing the fourth, and completing a 3–1 success in the rubber with another victory in the final match at The Oval.

Before these events began to unfold Denis had some modest scores against Glamorgan and Yorkshire. Glamorgan, I might add, were the only county whose bowlers denied him a hundred throughout his career, although it must be said that he faced them only rarely. The Yorkshire match, which was watched by almost 30,000 spectators on the Saturday, was notable within the context of this book for a highly unusual dismissal which involved Denis in his second innings.

Pinned down by some tight bowling from Bob Appleyard, Denis became so restless that the Yorkshire off-spinner/cutter anticipated correctly that the first ball of his new over would have Denis advancing down the pitch before he let it go. Changing his grip to hold the ball loosely in his hand, Bob let him have a 'beamer' directed absolutely on target at the batsman's head. Most batsmen confronting such a totally unexpected delivery, with precious little time to pick up its line and length, would have been happy somehow to avoid being hit. Not Denis, who had the flexibility to fashion a hook shot. The ball hit him on a glove and, remarkably enough, Don Brennan, the highly talented Yorkshire wicket keeper, who was standing up to the stumps, took the catch.

The deliberate 'beamer' has been regarded as being contrary to the

109

spirit of the game. Bob Appleyard tells me that at the time of this event there was much talk about it being employed by John Warr for Middlesex, although Bob soon came to realise that it was merely an excuse for 'J.J.' to extend his repertoire in a witty after-dinner speech. Anyway, Bob says it was the only 'beamer' he ever bowled, and he came to regret it. Yorkshire's players thought it, at the time, a good deal more amusing than Denis, who was much put out in more ways than one.

It is interesting how an event of this kind can become embellished down the years. I am told by a distinguished Yorkshire cricketer, who was not even playing in the match, that Denis and Bob had a somewhat fierce altercation as a number of 'beamers' were sent down, and that it was some while before amicable relations were restored. Yet, Bob, as I have said, felt remorse for having delivered just one. 'As a Yorkshireman I was unfamiliar with such unorthodoxy and improvisation, but I grew to respect and admire the skill and charisma of a superstar. What a genius!' I might add that the brush he had with Denis occurred in his first full season, when he took exactly 200 wickets and headed the national averages. He was a very fine bowler not blessed with robust health.

It was a promising toss for Brown to win in the second Test at Lord's. England scored an enterprising 311 on the first day before heavy rain provided a pitch fully exploited by Roy Tattersall. The Lancashire off-spinner took twelve wickets for 101 runs as South Africa were put out for 115 and 211. England then got 16 for no wicket to win conclusively.

After a sprightly beginning Denis again had to work hard for his runs, 79, before he was leg before to McCarthy. In the middle of England's effort Mann with his left-arm slow bowling had a spell of twenty-four overs for only 28. This, as it happened, was the last innings Denis played for three weeks. A foot turned septic from a blow on the toe. He was unfit for the third Test at Old Trafford where his place was taken by Tom Graveney, a young batsman of obvious potential.

When England won the third Test in Manchester by nine wickets – a victory looking more comfortable on paper than in fact it was – Len Hutton finished the match with 98 not out, just short of what would have been his hundredth hundred. The milestone was attained five days later, against Surrey at The Oval, which seemed, as it was not in Yorkshire, an appropriate venue for someone who had set a memorable record there in 1938. It was left to Geoffrey Boycott, twenty-six years later against Australia, to accomplish the feat on a Test match stage in front of his own supporters.

Bedser took seven for 58 at Old Trafford as South Africa were bowled out in their first innings for 158. To this, in testing conditions, England replied with 211 but Bedser did the trick again, in the tourists' second innings, with another five wickets, and Hutton steered England to a 2–1 lead in the series.

None the worse for an interlude, Denis now took up again more or less as he had left off. First he got 113 and 60 not out against Essex at Colchester. Next, captaining the Players against the Gentlemen, he hit a chanceless 150 out of 232 in three and a half hours, and followed it with 74 not out in the second innings. But he failed twice against Surrey at The Oval, and more significantly he missed the boat on his return to the England side.

The fourth Test at Headingley was laid to rest as a draw shortly after England had replied with 505 to South Africa's 538 on a lifeless pitch. Peter May signalled his arrival on the international scene with 138, Hutton got exactly 100, Bailey 95. But Denis, who fell lbw to Athol Rowan for only 25, had even less joy in the field where he dropped three catches off Bedser in the space of two overs. He got the bird after that, being booed every time he touched the ball. Eric Rowan, by then the cornerstone of South Africa's batting, ground his way to a score of 236. Denis cannot now recall a single shot he played. It was not a match he remembers with any special warmth.

As it turned out, the hundred he had made for the Players, the only one he hit in twenty-five innings against the Gentlemen, was his last of the summer. But there was no serious decline in his touch and he rose to the occasion with a brilliant 97 in Jack Parker's benefit match at The Oval.

The final Test was the best match of the series. It was played on a good cricket wicket and the result could have gone either way. South Africa made 202 and 154, England 194 and 164 for six to win by four wickets and to take the series 3–1. Denis scored 73, top score on either side, and yet again showed a gritty and determined side to his batting.

The last innings of the game was the one in which, for the only time in the history of Test cricket, a batsman was given out for 'obstructing the field'. Instinctively seeking to protect his stumps from a rebound via his glove and forearm, Len Hutton impeded the wicket keeper's attempted catch. The bowler, Athol Rowan, got no credit for the dismissal on the scoresheet.

In his second innings Denis made 18 before being caught off Geoffrey Chubb, a bespectacled, mild-looking medium pacer whose 21 wickets in the series were exceeded only by Bedser with 30 (for the second time in one year). For Chubb it was a case of Test life beginning and ending fruitfully at the age of 40. It was his only series.

Denis ended his successful summer with a whirlwind 84 for an England XI against the South Africans at Hastings for a final first-class tally of 2,193 runs at 64.50 In the Middlesex championship averages he stood second to the consistent, ever-cultured Jack Robertson, who enjoyed his finest season with 2,917 runs. Middlesex, without Denis for all but half of their matches, finished seventh. The county champions were Warwickshire, led by Ted Dollery.

Denis now took the winter off for the first time since joining the staff at Arsenal and Lord's in 1932/33. Arsenal had made him a life member at Highbury when his football career came to an end. Now he had the chance to go racing on Saturday afternoons, to relax and, I dare say, to put on some weight.

1952: Dropped by England

DENIS LOOKS BACK ON 1952 as having been his least satisfying season although he began it well enough, and it marked the occasion when he reached the 100th century of his first-class career. But it was also the one in which he was left out of the England side, for the first time in eleven years, for a reason other than injury.

The month of May brought him two hundreds, against Worcestershire and Leicestershire, as well as some other good scores. These were followed by 85 in Jack Young's benefit match, against Sussex, in the traditional Whitsun encounter at Lord's. It was time now for a new Test series to begin, against India, whose victory over England in Madras the previous winter, their first at international level, had enabled them to share the rubber with an MCC side a long way below full strength. In those days England could afford to visit the subcontinent without many of their luminaries. Some outstanding bowlers were happy to give India's lifeless pitches a miss.

In England in 1952 the Indians found themselves outgunned and outclassed in the first three Test matches, and only the weather in a miserable summer saved them in the last. Len Hutton, the first professional cricketer to be appointed England's captain, therefore missed a clean sweep.

The Headingley Test, which England won by seven wickets, will be for ever remembered for the scoreboard showing India in their second innings to have lost their first four wickets for no runs. A tempestuous young fast bowler, name of Fred Trueman, accounted for three of them in eight balls – not a bad start to his international career.

There was no way back for India after that. They were bowled out for 165, having made 293 in their first innings, Vijay Manjreker getting a polished 133. England's scores were 293 and 165. Denis struggled to make 14 in his first innings before being caught at short leg off a talented off-spinner, Ghulam Ahmed, but he finished with 35 not out in his second as England moved prudently towards a modest target.

Two days later he became the fourteenth cricketer to join a hall of enduring fame. The setting for his hundredth hundred, appropriately enough, was Lord's, and the team which made him work hard for it (107) was the same one, Northamptonshire, off whom he had taken his first in 1936. It was fitting, too, that Bill Edrich should have been in with him when the milestone was reached. Denis got there in 552 innings. Don Bradman (295) is the only batsman to have done so faster.

It should be mentioned at this point that India had arrived in England without their outstanding all-rounder, Vinoo Mankad, who had opted to play instead for Haslingden in the Lancashire League. His differences with the Indian Board were now resolved to the extent that he made himself available for the three remaining Test matches, and he lost no time in making a considerable impact. Going in first at Lord's, he made 72 and 184, and still had stamina left to bowl 97 overs for 231 runs and five first innings wickets. But this durable, versatile performance failed to save India from another decisive defeat.

To India's first innings of 235 England replied with 537, Hutton accelerating to a sumptuous 150 and Evans (104) going even faster with 98 before lunch on the third day. May and Graveney got attractive 70s but Denis failed, falling lbw to Hazare for 6. England eventually made heavy weather of the 76 they required in the last innings, and Denis, no happier with his form, remained 4 not out when they won by eight wickets.

For the first time in his England career Denis felt unequal to the job. He took counsel with Walter Robins, and it was agreed that he should write to the chairman of selectors asking to be left out. This letter, when duly publicised, produced some unpleasant reaction, it being suggested that it was always a good thing to get in first when a man knew he was due for the axe. Denis says he wanted to make certain that he was dropped. On the whole he got a poor press that summer, mostly, he recalls, from those he thought knew very little about the game. Jack Ikin, the sturdy Lancashire left-hander, took over from him in the third Test, and Denis returned full-time to the Middlesex camp for the rest of the summer.

There was no respite for India. Undone by Trueman's fire at Headingley, they had even less liking for him at Old Trafford where he had a green pitch to exploit and a howling gale at his back. He swept through some distinctly apprehensive opposition to take eight wickets for 31. Bedser and Lock took the honours in the second innings and India, bowled out for 58 and 82, went down by an innings and 207 runs. Hutton had got another hundred (104) in an England total of 347. Evans had made a brisk 71 to add to that century at Lord's and his 66 at Headingley. England's wicketkeeper was enjoying a buoyant series.

In the last Test at The Oval, England, having declared at 326 for six (Hutton 86, David Sheppard 119), bowled out India for 98 but not another ball was sent down after Hutton had asked them to bat again. In their second innings India lost their first five wickets for 6 runs. Bedser and Trueman shared all ten of the Indian wickets, England's mettlesome fast bowler finishing his first (four-match) Test series with 26 victims at 13.31. Hutton (399 runs at 79.80) dominated the batting averages.

Denis thought the choice of Len Hutton as captain was a good one but he confessed in *Playing for England* that he knew the captain's way of playing cricket would not be his. He was unimpressed by the tedious rate of progress made by England's opening batsmen at The Oval, when the series had been already decided. He also considered that the heady wine of early success was too much for Fred Trueman who believed his press and took a long time to listen to the advice of older hands.

When Denis returned to the Middlesex side after the Lord's Test match he first got 82 at Gloucester, without being able to impose his authority. He then failed twice against Hampshire, on each occasion being dismissed by the medium-pace bowler, Vic Cannings, who often got him out, but then made 90 and 55 against Essex at Colchester. His first innings there took an hour and three-quarters, which does not suggest that he was struggling to rediscover his form and confidence. 'He was racing to a hundred before lunch,' Trevor Bailey recollects, 'so I thought I'd try some leg theory. The runs suddenly dried up completely. Then I bowled him with a round-armer behind his legs. He was not best pleased.'

Denis by now had already sent off that letter to the chairman of selectors, and hardly anything occurred during the rest of the season to suggest that he had made a mistaken decision. In his next eighteen championship innings he reached 50 only once, got past 40 five times but was otherwise unsuccessful. There were some better performances towards the end of the season when he made 71 in his best style on a dusty, wearing pitch against Lancashire at Lord's, and 132 in three hours for an England XI against the Indians at Hastings.

Roly Jenkins remembers Denis's last innings that season well: 11 for the South against the Rest of England. 'The South wickets were going down so fast in their first innings, I was worried if there'd be any play for the customers to watch on the third day. When Denis came in to face me, I said, "Whatever you do, don't get out." And he said, "Don't worry. Bowl decently, and you'll never get me out." I pitched a near

115

long hop two feet outside the leg stump, and clean bowled him. It's the only time I ever had his wicket, and I really wasn't trying to get him out.'

Surrey, under the dynamic leadership of Stuart Surridge, won the first of their record seven successive championships in 1952. Middlesex finished fifth, an improvement on the previous season, but they suffered a decline in the second half of the summer to which Denis's lack of form contributed. His sharing of the captaincy with Bill Edrich had now run its unsatisfactory course for two years. Edrich took sole charge the following season.

This was the year when John Murray, then just seventeen, made his debut for Middlesex. At that stage of his career he was regarded primarily as a batsman, but got his first chance as a wicket keeper when Leslie Compton had back trouble. Standing back to Alan Moss, Murray blithely collected a ball down the off side and, *à la* Godfrey Evans, in one and the same motion shovelled it in the direction of Denis at first slip, for subsequent return to the bowler. By then, unhappily, Denis had resumed conversation with second slip, and the ball hit him on the back of his head. He was not at all impressed.

'In those early days,' Murray says, 'I found Compo intolerant and not very helpful, although Bill [Edrich] was always encouraging. I remember Denis in 1952 ordering me to take my time getting to the wicket when we played Yorkshire at Bramall Lane. I got booed. So did Denis who I think had written something about Len Hutton which wasn't well received in the Dales. I can tell you that if Denis and Bill were almost solely bent on entertainment in their later years, against Yorkshire and Surrey it was something different.' For his part, until he got used to it, Denis found Murray's air of jaunty confidence irritating. But they got on well together after Murray returned to the Middlesex side from military service.

In spite of all his problems Denis still managed to head the Middlesex championship batting averages, and to make 1,880 runs overall at 39.16. He also had his most productive summer as a bowler, taking 77 wickets at 28.58. A lot of players would have been happy to finish with such an all-round return.

1953: The Ashes Regained At Last

WHEN THE Australian touring team, captained by Lindsay Hassett, sailed into Southampton in April 1953 there seemed reasonable cause for optimism in the home country that England had the capacity to beat them. The victory gained by Freddie Brown's side at the end of the 1950/51 series in Australia had signalled a recovery. In batting, at least, the old enemy looked as if they might be vulnerable. Moreover, they arrived in a wet summer without an orthodox specialist spin bowler. But Lindwall, Miller and Johnston, not exactly in their dotage yet, were back again and the presence in the side of three newcomers, Alan Davidson, Richie Benaud and Ron Archer, represented a more than useful all-round strength.

The bare record of four drawn matches followed by a win for England in the last Test suggests a satisfying climax for the home team but a not very dramatic series as a whole. The truth was different. In three of the four drawn games the fortunes of both sides waxed or waned in turn. In the second of them, England needed a now historic rearguard action by Willie Watson and Trevor Bailey to avoid defeat. In the fourth, they were looking down the barrel again when Bailey, who had previously held out as a batsman for more than four hours, saved the day with a spell of defensive bowling down the leg side.

Denis certainly was not alone in thinking little of Bailey's tactics used at Headingley, but they meant that England went on to The Oval still with a chance of winning the series and regaining the Ashes for the first time in nineteen years. Jim Laker and Tony Lock made the decisive thrust there, and the old Middlesex duo were in at the death when Denis made the winning hit and the crowd erupted joyfully on to the field. I still think that moment is the most emotive in my cricket experience.

The English success represented a personal triumph for Len Hutton who not only led the batting averages with 443 runs at 55.37 but became the first captain to win a Test series after losing the toss in every match. It was no less a *tour de force* for Alec Bedser, who set a new record with 39 wickets, and for Bailey, whose all-round contribution was crucial. Denis played four good innings without once extending them into something really substantial. For him a rather ordinary series could not wholly be explained away by physical limitations although these contributed to his missing several chances close-in. The time had come for him to field further out.

After a second successive winter at home he began the season encouragingly enough, with a hundred for Middlesex in a tied match at Northampton. Then, later in May, he got 2 and 45 for MCC against the Australians, in his first innings being lbw on the back foot to a slower ball from Lindwall after that bowler had disposed of Reg Simpson and David Sheppard for 0 apiece. In his second, he was given out leg before again, this time padding up to Davidson. Bailey subsequently scored 64 not out in three hours; by the end of the summer the Australians were sick of the sight of him.

In his next county fixture, on his 35th birthday, Denis did Sid Brown proud in his benefit match with a dashing 143 and, three games later, took 109 off Yorkshire's attack at Lord's. This seemed adequate preparation for the first Test match which followed at Trent Bridge, but in his one innings there Denis registered 0. He chased an outswinger from Lindwall that was well wide of the off stump, and Arthur Morris held on to a splendid catch in the gully.

Although it was much affected by rain and played almost throughout in dank conditions, this first Test match riveted attention throughout its course. The new ball was used to such effect by Bedser that he twice took seven wickets in an innings for an aggregate of 99 runs. Australia were first bowled out for 249, from a one-time pinnacle of 237 for three, and 123.

A devastating spell from Lindwall reduced England to 17 for three wickets in their first innings, with Don Kenyon, Reg Simpson and Compton all falling to him. They were eventually all out for 144. Time then ran out for them in the last innings of the game. They finished up with 120 for one wicket, still 128 runs short of an impossible target. It was a moral victory for England, although it has to be said that Keith Miller was unable to bowl for Australia. In Australia's first innings Morris got 67, Hassett 115 and Miller 55. Morris, who had a fine match (60 in his second effort), fell on that occasion to his familiar *bête noire*, Bedser. But Bedser's *coup de main* was the unplayable ball with which he bowled Hassett – an inswinger which pitched on leg stump and hit the top of the off.

There was another moment for England to relish when Bedser had Neil Harvey (four hundreds in his last four matches against the counties) caught by Denis for 0 off a leg glance. 'Not a bad catch?' Denis enquired of the bowler. 'Wish you'd pick 'em up first time,' Alec said. 'You make me so bloody nervous.' But the most spectacular dismissal was that of Benaud, to a stupendous diving leg-side catch by Godfrey Evans off the bowling of Bailey. Denis has never seen a better Test match wicket-keeper than Evans, who was essentially a man for the big occasion.

Denis had one Middlesex game to play before the Test series was resumed, Andy Wilson's benefit in Bristol, in which he made 57. Tom Graveney says that Denis was the only person to make batting look a simple business on an impossible pitch.

Does anyone seriously believe that a drawn game cannot be as excit-ing as one that is won or lost? The second Test, which veered first to one side's advantage and then to the other's, came to a gripping climax as Watson and Bailey for England confounded all gloomy predictions. But first things first.

There was little in it on first innings. Australia made 346, their dapper captain getting another hundred (104) and Bedser taking another five wickets. England replied with 372, in which Hutton made 145 – perhaps the best Test century of his career – Graveney 78 and Denis 57. It was disappointing that England did not get more, since they were 279 for two at one point in their innings. But there was some batting of rare quality in its earlier stages, including the pleasure of a partnership of 102 shared by Hutton and Compton.

They needed to be on their mettle against a hectic assault from Lindwall and Miller, Denis remembering it as being the fastest bowling he had faced at that stage of his career. The fur was flying when his captain called him for a word between wickets at the end of an over. 'There must be a better way,' Len said, 'of earning a bluddy living.' Denis was going well when he pushed out to a leg-break from Benaud, to be caught at slip.

Keith Miller was to have a modest series by his exalted all-round standards but he got 109 in Australia's second innings, he and Morris threatening England with a daunting task to come when Denis had the left-hander spectacularly caught for 89 by Brian Statham off a long hop. Lindwall struck a rapid 50 in the lower order before Australia were all out again, for 368. England had not helped themselves by putting down eight chances, three of which had to be marked against the name of the captain.

In *The Fight for the Ashes 1953* I wrote, 'I doubt if one cricketer in a hundred seriously gave a fig for the English chances at the end of the fourth day's play, when the wickets of Hutton, Kenyon and Graveney had been lost for 12 runs. With a whole day's play to come, with the pitch wearing and the weather set fair, it seemed that only a miracle could save England. The miracle was achieved . . . and it was Compton's splendid innings which showed the way.'

All went well next morning, the score being advanced by 52 runs in the first hour, until Denis fell lbw for 33 to a ball from Bill Johnston that swung in and kept indecently low. That brought in Bailey to join Watson, who was playing his first Test against Australia. Their heroic partnership lasted for four and a quarter hours before Watson was caught at slip off Doug Ring for 109. In that leg-spinner's next over Bailey (71) was taken at backward point. England 246 for six, with thirty-five minutes to go.

Clearly there was still time for Australia to win, but the chairman of England's selectors, Freddie Brown, who had been chosen by his colleagues to play in one last Test match, launched a characteristically robust attack on Ring and Benaud. A memorable game of cricket ended with England on 282 for seven. 'If we get another Test match like this,' Sir Donald Bradman observed as he left the press box, 'I shan't be able to stand the strain.'

Denis now got a fifty against Essex at Lord's before winning the game for Middlesex with five wickets for 58 in the last innings, his brother Leslie then claiming six victims. The resumption of the Test rubber at Old Trafford saw a match reduced by the weather to less than fourteen hours of play. It ended with Australia, who were left just fifty minutes to bat in the third innings, reduced by Laker and Wardle to 35 for eight. Wardle finished with four for 7. Some of the batting looked distinctly light-hearted.

Bedser added to his impressive haul of wickets with five more in an Australian first innings of 318 to which Neil Harvey contributed his only hundred of the series. England's reply of 276 was lit by another Hutton/Compton partnership of rare pedigree on a drying pitch. Hutton got 66 and Denis 45 before being caught behind off Archer when playing quietly for stumps towards the end of Saturday's play. There was no play at all on the Monday.

At one point during that third Test match, during a stoppage for bad light, Keith Miller joined Denis for a game of cards in England's dressing room. Denis says that Len Hutton raised his eyebrows. The captain was not too sure that such fraternisation was timely.

For the Players against the Gentlemen, Denis managed only 13 and 0, on both occasions falling to the Cambridge and Sussex off-spinner Robin Marlar. He then got another duck in his first innings of the fourth Test at Headingley, when he steered an inswinger from Lindwall quite gently to leg slip. He was in good company; Hutton was yorked second ball by Lindwall for a similar score.

These misfortunes occurred after England had been put in to bat by Australia for the first time since 1909. The opening day's play produced the paltry return of 142 for seven wickets off 90 overs in more than five and a half hours. Australia, who were to hold the initiative throughout this encounter, subsequently replied with 266, a first innings lead of 99. With six more wickets, Bedser surpassed Clarrie Grimmett's Test record of 216.

England, now up against it, got their noses in front with only two wickets down whereupon, after a slump in mid-innings, Bailey held the fort yet again (as previously recorded) and Laker got a very handy 48. England were bowled out for 275, Bill Edrich having made 64 and Denis an equally combative 61. Denis was batting in considerable difficulty on the penultimate evening, having been struck a painful blow by Lindwall on the left hand. Unable to hold a bat on the last morning, he eventually – thanks to a pain-killing injection – resumed soon after lunch when England were 239 for seven, only 140 in front.

Before he had added to his score Denis edged a ball from Lindwall to first slip where Graeme Hole triumphantly claimed a catch. Denis, not satisfied that the ball had carried, stood his ground and waited for the umpire's decision. Frank Lee, who was unsighted at the bowler's end, referred the matter to Frank Chester at square-leg. 'It was bloody well not out,' Denis has reported Chester as saying. As it happened, he *was* out, lbw Lindwall, very soon after this incident. The Australians later refused to have Frank Chester standing in the final Test.

In the last innings of the Headingley match Australia needed 177 to win in an hour and fifty-five minutes. Len Hutton, recalling their struggles against the turning ball at Old Trafford and sensing the possibility of an England win, opened his attack with Bedser and Lock. But the plan misfired. Lock was struck for 48 runs in eight overs as Australia went at it hell for leather. When Davidson joined Hole, only three wickets having fallen, they needed only another 66 in forty-five minutes.

It was at this critical point, while Bedser continued to hold the other end, that Bailey was brought on. For six overs, off the longest run he might decently employ, his one wicket for 9 runs saved England's bacon. His attack was concentrated wide of the leg stump to a thickly populated leg-side field. There was no slip. It was not a pretty sight. Australia, 147 for four at the finish, were held off. 'Trevor made it possible for

England to win back the Ashes,' Denis has said. 'But I think it was unfair and should never have been done. It wasn't cricket. The Aussies were furious. Their anger was justified.' This was the only occasion in an otherwise thoroughly happy series when feathers were genuinely ruffled.

In his three games for Middlesex before the fifth Test Denis hit 70s against Sussex and Kent, and his fourth hundred of the summer, 113, against Surrey. He seemed to be in good form for the climax to the rubber, but his part in that long-awaited English triumph was, except at the death, undistinguished. He scored 16 and 22 not out, Lindwall having him caught at the wicket down the leg side. The great Australian bowler has always held that, if there was a chink in Denis's armour, it lay in his tendency to play the leg glance with his bat outside the leading pad. It is of interest that Lindwall got his wicket (13 times) more than any other bowler. Alec Bedser and Bill Johnston each had it on twelve occasions, Hugh Tayfield on ten.

In the final Test, England did the trick at last in just four days, although by mutual agreement the match could have run to a sixth. There was little in it on first innings, Australia making 275 and England 306, 82 of them from Hutton and 64 from – who else? – Bailey in almost four hours. Fred Trueman, in his only match of the series, earned his spurs with four wickets.

On the third day Australia were 59 for one in their second innings when Laker and Lock achieved the vital breakthrough with four wickets for two runs. The lower batting order made a fight of it, but, without ever relaxing their grip, the Surrey spinners bowled out Australia for 162. Lock had five wickets for 45, Laker four for 75. England were left to make 132 with more than two days to spare.

It was shortly before 3 o'clock on the Monday afternoon, England 9 runs short of their target, that Hassett signalled surrender by bowling an over himself. He told his vice-captain, Arthur Morris, to be ready to send down the next. 'Don't get the runs off Lindsay,' Morris said to Denis. 'I want to be on television for the next 100 years.' Denis took the hint and, when Arthur bowled him a genial left-arm long hop, helped it down to the gasholder at long leg for the winning runs.

Bedser with his record 39 wickets in the series, at 17.48, dominated England's bowling averages just as Hutton did the batting ones. Lindwall (26 at 18.84) was way out top of Australia's bowlers. Denis got 234 runs at 33.42.

He had three days to recover from celebrating England's success before going back to The Oval for the return match between Surrey and Middlesex. Arthur Morris, not engaged with the Australians at the time, was a spectator on the second day. 'It was fascinating,' he recalls, 'to watch Compton and Edrich on a very nasty wet pitch. Bill really struggled. Denis was superb. He flayed the bowling. It was beautiful stuff. When I got back to base, I said to our fellows, "Thank God he doesn't play like that in Test matches – he'd kill us." But of course he was a magnificent Test cricketer.'

The all-rounder Don Bennett, now county coach, was in the Middlesex side then. He thinks that 63, made out of 77 in fifty minutes, was the best innings he ever saw Denis play. 'It was against bowling of the highest class on a pig of a pitch. It was impossible to play forward.'

Denis came down to earth with 0 (his fourth that summer) and 2 against Lancashire. He finished his 1953 summer with 81, in two hours, for South of England against the Australians at Hastings, and an aggregate of 1,659 runs in all first-class matches.

Middlesex, for whom a young off-spinner, Fred Titmus, was playing his first full season, again promised more than they finally achieved. They retained fifth place in the championship, after heading the table for much of the summer. The old firm still stood atop their team's championship averages: Edrich 1,748 runs at 47.24, Compton (in seven fewer games) 1,098 at 43.92. But after seven highly productive summers Jack Robertson suffered a marked decline in form.

Victory in the Test series was not the only source of English joy in 1953. This was the year when Jack Hobbs, acknowledged master on all wickets, was knighted.

1953/54: In the Caribbean

WEST INDIES had won in England in 1950; England had beaten Australia in 1953. *Ergo*, West Indies *v* England, 1953/54, could be seen as a world championship. It was sad that the series in the Caribbean was seen in that light. The fact that West Indies had been roundly defeated, 4–1, in Australia in 1951/52 was conveniently forgotten.

Much of the England tour was played against a background of racial tension, of volatile crowds who twice rioted in oppressive heat, of a conviction on the part of the visitors that the Test umpiring was incompetent and biased, and of incidents on and off the field which a loyal English press contingent did their best to play down. In those days there were no purely news reporters sent out to make the most of such events and to dig up what further dirt they could find. More crucially, no doubt, there was no television to bring every unsavoury incident into the parlours of the cricket world.

In spite of everything the relationship between the opposing players, a few brouhahas apart, remained good. The last Test was conducted in a traditionally civilised atmosphere, and Len Hutton's side did thoroughly well, after an indifferent start to the series, to square the series after they had been two matches down. The captain had a magnificent tour as batsman, scoring 677 runs in the Test matches at a princely average of 96.71, but Denis was not alone amongst his colleagues in believing that, as a leader, Hutton in the early part of the series put far too great an emphasis on a defensive approach.

He has written that his captain, by remaining aloof and declining to mix socially off the field, contributed to a poor image of the team as ambassadors. Denis, who accepts his share of the blame for that, also thought that Hutton should have brought Trueman to heel much sooner than he did.

The fiery Fred gave regular rein to his temper with a series of predictable if unvarying expletives, all of which tended to keep the tinder crackling. Reg Hayter, a respected reporter covering the tour in *Wisden*, wrote that Hutton was anxious not to dim the spark of Trueman's natural hostility and aggression. When Denis was briefly in charge of MCC against Barbados, he told Trueman that if he didn't behave himself he would do his best to have him sent home on the next boat. Frederick apparently took due notice of the threat.

A schedule of fixtures imposing no discomforts on MCC had them beginning their tour with two first-class games, in which Denis made 56 and 47, against Jamaica. But in the first Test, at Sabina Park in Kingston, he managed only 12 and 2. England lost it by 140 runs.

They thought the Test pitch, which looked like shining marble, would be a fast one. So they picked four seam bowlers – Statham, Trueman, Moss and Bailey – supported by one specialist spinner, Lock. It did not play at all as expected, and in the circumstances England did well enough to restrict West Indies to a first innings total of 417. The top score of 94 was made by a Jamaican, J. K. Holt, jnr., whose father had toured England in 1923. A section of the crowd was so incensed by the umpire's decision when Holt was given out lbw to Statham that the umpire's wife and son were physically assaulted though, happily, without lasting harm.

England's performance in their first innings, their batsmen held in thrall by Ramadhin and Valentine, seemed like a replay of the events in England in 1950. Between them that duo sent down sixty-six overs for 115 runs and seven wickets. England were bowled out for a miserable 170, but the West Indies' captain, Jeff Stollmeyer, did not enforce the follow-on. Having been roundly booed for this decision he eventually declared their second innings closed at 209 for six with Everton de Courcey Weekes 90 not out. England were left nine and a half hours to score an almost unreachable 457 in the last innings of the match.

They set off on a daunting task successfully enough to inspire a hope of something remarkable. At close of play on the penultimate evening they were 227 for two, the outfield being lightning fast. Willie Watson (116) and Len Hutton (56) led the way with a confident opening partnership of 130. However, Stollmeyer tactically shut up shop on the last day. Just before lunch May was caught down the leg side for 69 and, shortly after it, Denis failed again. The only meaningful resistance then came from Graveney (34) and Bailey (15), who had made an undefeated 28 in the first innings and batted for three and a half hours in the match without losing his wicket. England were all out for 316.

Denis had been lbw to Valentine in the first innings. After his second failure, this time to Ramadhin, Alex Bannister reported in the *Daily Mail* 'that Denis Compton, whose Test career must be rapidly drawing to its close, left the widest of gaps between bat and pad in pushing forward defensively to an off-break from Ramadhin which turned appreciably – one of the few balls in the match which did'. We all make inaccurate forecasts, even someone as knowledgeable as Bannister.

This island game in Barbados, in which MCC had an exciting victory by one wicket, was chiefly notable for three things. Denis Atkinson introduced himself to the tourists with a most dashing 151; Tony Lock was called three times for throwing by the umpire Harold Walcott – uncle of Clyde – and did not bowl his fast ball on tour again; and Hutton, batting at number 8 with a nasty chill on his liver, hit a quite brilliant 59 not out. Denis, still struggling to find his best form, made 41 and 15.

England's batting was no more exciting in the second Test at Kensington Oval in Bridgetown, Barbados. Winning the toss again, West Indies began with an innings of 383 which was dominated by Walcott's 220 after England had taken their first three wickets for 25. England then occupied five hours of play on the third day by grinding out 128 runs for seven wickets off 114 overs, the captain getting 72 of them in half an hour less. Denis kept his nose to the official grindstone in making 13. In the morning, on a good pitch, Ramadhin was permitted to bowl seventeen overs for 12 runs, and Valentine nineteen for 14.

It is interesting to reflect that with Ramadhin and Valentine still calling their tune, West Indies got through their overs at almost 23 an hour. These days they seem hard pushed to average little more than half as much as they rotate their battery of fast bowling.

West Indies, declining once again to enforce the follow-on, increased their first innings lead of 202 to 494 before Stollmeyer declared at 292 for two in which J. K. Holt hit a punishing 166. England had to bat for nine and a half hours to save the game. On this occasion, after representations had been made to the skipper, their approach was refreshingly different. Hutton got 72, May 62, and shortly after lunch on the last day, when Denis was 7 runs short of a vigorous hundred, England were 258 for three and poised, perhaps, to make a draw of it.

At that point he stretched a long way forward to a googly from Stollmeyer and was given out lbw. Graveney, who was in with him at the time, says it was just about the worst decision he has ever seen. It turned the game. The last seven wickets fell for 55 runs, and West Indies went two-up in the rubber with a win by 181 runs. Denis walked off without demur.

From Barbados MCC moved to the mainland for the third Test, in Georgetown. This was preceded by a match against British Guiana in which Watson (257) and Graveney (231) made 402 for the fourth wicket.

England then proceeded to signal their recovery in the rubber with a win over West Indies by nine wickets, but not before the crowd had run amok in one of the two riots which so scarred the series.

After Hutton had won the toss for the only time in the rubber he stroked a flawless 169 in an England total of 435. Denis contributed the next highest score of 64. Brian Statham then ripped out the wickets of Worrell, Stollmeyer and Walcott at a personal cost of 10 runs and, although Weekes hit a thunderous 94, England looked set for a substantial lead only to be held up by McWatt and Holt's stand of 99 for the eighth wicket.

At that moment, the rum flowing and many a bet having been laid in the crowd that a century stand would be achieved, McWatt was run out by a swift return from May. None of the players was in any doubt that the umpire made a good decision, but the crowd erupted, throwing bottles and heaven knows what else on to the field.

It was a menacing turn in events but one of Hutton's finest hours. 'I want another couple of wickets tonight,' he said, and stood his ground. After order had been restored, he got one, that of Ramadhin, who did not fancy the situation at all. 'Give me a straight one,' he told Laker, 'and you can have mine.' When the stumps were pulled out that evening, umpire Menzies is said to have created a local sprint record in his dash for the pavilion and safety. Next morning, England bowled out West Indies for 251 and, in the follow-on, for 256.

It was a good win and it sent them rejoicing to Trinidad, where they had the satisfaction of becoming the only touring team to defeat all four colony sides. Denis got 90 in his second innings there, much of it in company with Bailey who went in first to make a similar score with an uncharacteristically stirring display of stroke play. At one stage Bailey said to his partner, 'I want you to stay there, Compo, while I play the shots', and turned his back on him before Compo had time to think of a suitable reply.

No one had any doubt that the fourth Test would be drawn, as it was to be played on the Port of Spain's jute matting. All three of the well-known Ws got hundreds in a West Indian total of 681 for eight declared, Walcott helping himself to a doubleton with some fearsome strokes. England then replied with 537, May making 135 and Denis 133 – his first Test hundred for almost three years – and Graveney 92. West Indies declared their second innings closed at 212 for four, and the match was quietly laid to rest, as had been universally predicted, with England on 98 for three. That made for an overall aggregate of 1,528 runs for only twenty-five wickets.

There had been, alas, two combustible events on the first day. The second occurred after Denis had come on to break West Indies' opening partnership by having Stollmeyer caught and bowled. In the last over before lunch, he bowled a googly (turning away from the batsman) which Holt aimed to drive past cover. Graveney had spotted the wrong'un and was well prepared for the edged shot which in the opinion of all fielders within range palpably carried waist high to slip.

Tom threw the ball up and marched off for his meal. But Holt stayed put. Graveney then heard Hutton, at mid-off, saying to the umpire, Ellis Achong, 'Well, how was that, Ellis?' Achong was a former West Indies slow left-arm bowler. Denis, at mid-on, pursued the theme by saying, 'It's obvious Mr Holt edged it, and Tom caught it. Isn't he out?' 'No,' the umpire replied. 'Mr Holt is not out. The ball touched the ground first.' 'Dear, dear me,' Denis replied. (Denis reported his commendable restraint in one of his own books.)

Graveney's reaction was a good deal less diplomatic. Denis has quoted him as saying, 'How the hell do you get these — out?' Tom himself remembers throwing the ball on the ground in his temper, saying to Holt that this was the fourth time he had cheated England on tour, and marching off to a rare cacophony. Denis recalls it as being the only time in his career that he left the field with boos ringing in his ears. He did not enjoy the experience. But the crowd was outraged and so was Achong, who subsequently filed a complaint. The local media made the most of it, as they had every right to do.

This was not the only thing that upset England's fielders in that innings. Weekes was given not out caught behind off Bailey when they all thought the batsman had hit the ball hard. They made their disappointment clear enough, and Denis made a sarcastic comment to the umpire which he later regretted.

Whatever the pressures, it was no time for the representatives of MCC and England to be seen and portrayed as poor sportsmen. Let no one think that what Mike Gatting's side endured in Pakistan in 1987/88 had no previous parallel, or that old cricketers now prone to deplore a decline in behaviour were always knights in shining armour in their playing days. It is a rare thing for touring sides to be wholly satisfied by the umpiring, even in England, where standards are unarguably highest. But good, bad or indifferent, it has to be lived with, without dissent.

England now had to win the last Test match, back in Jamaica, to level the series. Their confidence was not enhanced by the loss of yet another toss and the prospect of bowling out West Indies on what appeared to be another good pitch, still less by the absence of Statham, who was unfit. They decided to include all three of their spinners, Laker, Lock and Wardle, with Trueman and Bailey to open their attack. And it was Bailey, vice-captain of the side, who did the trick by taking seven wickets for 34 runs in the first innings, the best performance of his Test career.

The Sabina Park groundsman had said it was the finest pitch he ever prepared. Yet Bailey on the first day was able to get a degree of swing, and he found just enough juice in the wicket to move the ball off the seam. West Indies were dismissed for 139 whereupon England, who could hardly believe what had happened, took command with a first innings of 414 to which their captain contributed a masterly 205 spread over all but nine hours. Denis was going well on 31, having just hooked King for two fours, when in attempting another he trod on his stumps.

England's long lead proved decisive. They bowled out West Indies again for 346, Walcott hitting his third hundred of the series, and then got the 72 they wanted for the loss of one wicket and with a day to spare.

This was the nineteenth and last time that Hutton passed three figures in Test cricket. But even his triumph at its climax was clouded by yet another unhappy incident. A weary Hutton, tunnel vision focused on his innings, did not realise that Jamaica's chief minister had touched his arm and congratulated him as he made his way through a crowded pavilion. Len had just arrived in the England dressing room when a government official barged in to say that this was 'the crowning insult'. England's captain was flabbergasted. He has written in his *Fifty Years in Cricket* that he had an evening drink with Mr Alex Bustamente, who assured him that he had not felt slighted and understood why he had not been recognised

This was also the Test match in which a promising all-rounder, Garfield St Aubrun Sobers, made his international debut. Batting at no.9, he made 14 not out and 26 as well as enjoying, in his (then) orthodox slow left-arm style, his side's most successful bowling figures, four for 75.

Denis had finished his tour, after a modest start, on a relatively high note. His knee had stood the strain remarkably well. He got 348 runs in the Test series, at 49.71, and 630 first-class runs all told at 48.46. In spite of its problems he loved almost every moment of his one and only England visit to the Caribbean, where the pitches in those days were made for batsmen and where he found the crowds knew more about the game than any others in the cricket world. He was fielding on the boundary in Georgetown when an old man said to him, 'Massa Weekes, Massa Worrell and Massa Walcott come first, and de Lawd above comes second.'

1954: Brilliant 278 *v* Pakistan

Denis was not seen at practice before Middlesex began a new championship season with a match against Hampshire at Lord's in early May. Nor, it seems, did he have a net on the first morning of the game. Lesser mortals might well have struggled after such a total lack of preparation, but this one made 117 and 64. Not only that, with his left-arm off-breaks and wrong' uns he took five for 19 and three for 58.

This exhilarating all-round performance was followed by another hundred, against Worcestershire, a fifty against Nottinghamshire and 82 against Gloucestershire, when Middlesex won their sixth consecutive match and threatened to turn the championship into a one-horse race. 'Bomber' Wells remembers seeing him advance down the pitch before he released the ball. 'Ah ha, I says to myself, you're going to get the quick one, Compo. It disappeared into the Gloucestershire dressing room behind long-off.' In the same innings Denis square cut George Lambert, fast medium, for six.

There were 20,000 spectators at Lord's for Leslie Compton's Benefit match against Sussex, played over the Whitsun week-end at Lord's. 'Big Les's' fate as a batsman in this encounter has previously been mentioned in a chapter devoted to his brother's occasional eccentricities between wickets. I should now add further details.

It is commonly believed these days that an abashed Denis, having confessed his guilt, then made a hundred for his brother by way of expiation. In fact, before the third day's play was lost, Middlesex (and Compton) ran out of time and were struggling to avoid defeat. Denis in his one innings made a masterly 72 not out on a rain-affected pitch. He also ran out Fred Titmus and Alan Moss. 'Don't worry about me,' said Moss, who came in at number 11 and was done with ease, 'You've got your not out.' Denis failed to appreciate the little joke.

He had begun his season with more than 500 runs in six completed innings. But the game of cricket, as has been observed so often, is the greatest leveller in the world. In the first Test match at Lord's he made nought, bowled by Fazal Mahmood.

It was Pakistan's misfortune, on their first tour of England, to run into what was said to have been the wettest English summer for fifty years. There was no play at Lord's on the first three days, and not much more than eight hours of it for the whole Test. Pakistan made 87

(Statham and Wardle sharing eight wickets) and 121 for three. England, who had won the toss, got 117 for nine declared. Fazal and Khan Mohammad bowled unchanged to claim four and five wickets respectively. All of Khan Mohammad's were clean bowled, including Hutton's with the first ball of the match. Another Mohammad, Hanif, who was then only 19, showed his defensive skills by batting almost six hours for 59 runs.

The story for England's batsmen was a very different one in the second Test match, at Trent Bridge, where they ran up a total of 558 for six declared. Denis made a remarkable 278, the highest score of his Test match career and, as it was to turn out, his last three-figure score at international level.

A handsome hundred by Reg Simpson, on his own Nottingham ground, was followed by a riveting partnership of 154 between Denis and Tom Graveney to which the pride of Gloucestershire contributed a flawlessly elegant 84. Trevor Bailey, happily conceding some 80 per cent of the strike to his partner, then shared in a stand of 192, of which Denis's share was 165, in one and three-quarter hours. Let *Wisden* take up the story of his progress '. . . with a torrent of strokes, orthodox and improvised, crashing and delicate, against which Kardar (Pakistan's captain) could not set a field, and the bowlers knew not where to pitch.'

Completing his second hundred in eighty minutes, Denis eventually was bowled having struck or caressed one six and thirty-three fours. The lad who bowled him was Khalid Hassan, a leg-spinner still thirteen days short of his seventeenth birthday – the then youngest debutant in Test match history – whose twenty-one overs went for 116 runs.

Fazal, one of the world's greatest medium-paced bowlers, had Denis very expensively missed, on 20. Pakistan, who batted first on winning the toss, made 157 and 272. Yorkshire's Bob Appleyard, with off-spin, cut and inswing signalled his arrival in England's side by taking four wickets for 6 runs in his opening spell. His captain in this and the third Test was David Sheppard, Len Hutton being unfit.

Before the Test rubber was resumed, in Manchester, Denis was involved in a game for Middlesex at Lord's which had a telling influence on the selection of a young fast bowler for next winter's tour of Australia. Frank Tyson, aged 24, was now in his first full season for Northants, having gravitated there via trials for Lancashire, his native county. No one by this time was in any doubt about his capacity to bowl intimidatingly fast.

Late on the first evening, the pitch lively and the light poor, the pugnacious Edrich, attempting to hook Tyson into the grandstand under old Father Time, was far too late with his stroke and suffered a sickening blow on the jaw. Tyson remembers how the blood on the pitch was covered with sawdust after Edrich had been carried off the field on a stretcher. Denis was due in next but, having taken an early bath, surveyed this dramatic turn in events from the Middlesex balcony with a towel draped around his middle. A young amateur, Peter Delisle, thus had the doubtful pleasure of facing the music on his first-class debut.

Remarkably, Bill Edrich was able to resume his innings next morning. His steadfast resistance did not last long, but Denis got a cavalier 55 and, in his second effort, another top score of 48. 'I was naive then,' Tyson recalls. 'My eyes almost popped out out of their sockets when I saw him coming down the pitch at me while I was half-way down my 25-yards run. As soon as I accepted the bait and dropped one short, he rocked back on his heels and hooked me for 6 almost into the arms of that well-known barracker, "Yorkshire Annie". The message was clear; no bowler, however fast, dictated terms to Denis Compton!'

Denis affirms that he never faced faster bowling than Tyson's in this match. At some time during its course he said, 'This fella will be just the ticket in Australia.'

At Old Trafford the weather once more played its miserable hand and play was limited to less than eleven hours on the first and third days. Pakistan certainly did not get the rub of the green. England made the most of winning the toss by reaching a total of 359 for eight declared in which Denis, still in prime fettle, made 93 out of 133 and Graveney stroked a princely 65. This was the innings when Bailey, who went in first to make 42, was run out by Denis in circumstances previously described. It seemed an unfortunate way for him to be repaid after his unselfish performance at Trent Bridge.

Pakistan were bowled out for 90 by Alec Bedser, Johnny Wardle and Jim McConnon, the Glamorgan off-spinner then making his debut. They were looking down the barrel, at 25 for four in their second innings, when the weather put an end to their troubles.

There was no decline in Denis's form when he got 63 and 101, in eighty-nine minutes, for Middlesex at Worcester. But at this stage of the season his knee flared up again and a touch of lumbago made things even more uncomfortable. Nor, in one respect, did England's selectors make things easier for themselves by leaving out Bedser and Bailey for the fourth and final Test at The Oval on a pitch which turned out to be well suited to them both. With an eye to the tour of Australia, the selectors brought in Tyson and Loader, each of whom did creditably enough. But Pakistan, on their first visit to this country, won an exciting Test match by just 24 runs, and squared the rubber as well.

There was very little in it on first innings, Pakistan making 133 and England just three runs more with Fazal taking six for 53. Johnny Wardle then took seven for 56 in thirty-five overs as Pakistan were bowled out for 164. Peter May, with a punitive 53, set England firmly on the road towards their goal of 168, but there was a slump in mid-innings and no reprieve on the final morning when Fazal's leg-cutters were too hot to withstand. Denis got top score of 53 in the first innings, being put down three times during a resistance lasting more than two hours, and 29 in his second. Fazal had him caught twice behind the wicket. The matchwinner was cheered into the pavilion with match figures of twelve for 99.

Denis finished that series with 453 runs at the exceptional average of 90.60. He also headed the first-class averages that season (1,524 runs at 58.61) but did not play again following the last Test match in mid-August. He had got his thousand in championship games for Middlesex – comfortably heading their averages, too – but the end to their season was far less successful than its start had been and they had to settle, equal with Northants, for seventh place.

1954/55: To Australia Again

THERE WERE SOME NOTABLE omissions from the passenger list when Len Hutton's side sailed out of Tilbury in September 1954 for the tour of Australia. No Trueman, no Laker or Lock – who between them bowled out Australia at The Oval in 1953 – and no D. C. S. Compton, whose bothersome knee delayed his departure by more than a month.

It said a lot for England's bowling resources at this time that their attack in Australia could still be spearheaded by Tyson, Statham, Bailey and Loader. They were supported by Wardle and two off-spinners, Appleyard and McConnon, the first named cutting the ball at almost medium pace. But advance planning held that on Australian pitches of the day the home side would be most vulnerable against pace. I should add that England's selectors also got it right in their choice of a young batsman, Colin Cowdrey, then 21, who had demonstrated his class and potential with Oxford University and Kent.

It was arranged for Denis to fly out to join the party in time for the South Australian match in Adelaide where MCC had arrived from Perth with two good first-class wins under their belts. His flight was notable for a hair-raising, belly-flop landing at Karachi after the nose wheel had failed to lower.

Composure restored by the time he arrived on Australian soil for his final cricket tour there, he declined the offer of a net and promptly made a quick 113. Against an Australian XI in Melbourne he got only 16, and he then missed the next fixture, with New South Wales in Sydney, where Cowdrey, batting at number 6, hit two hundreds off an attack which included Davidson, Miller and Benaud.

Promoted to open the innings against Queensland in a match preceding the first Test in Brisbane, Cowdrey did considerably less well with 4 and 0. Facing Lindwall on the tour for the first time MCC, in their first innings, were reduced to 18 for three but a stirring partnership between Reg Simpson (136) and Compton (110) improved matters. Denis subsequently made 69 in the second innings to suggest that he was in good order for the Test match.

Unfortunately for England's hopes and plans, on the eve of the Test match Godfrey Evans was taken ill and replaced by Keith Andrew. Discerning a pitch similar to that on which the Queensland game had been played, Hutton opted to go into this Test match with an all-seam attack and, on winning the toss, put Australia in to bat. The Australians ran up a total of 601 for eight declared, with Arthur Morris and Neil Harvey making big hundreds, and England spilling catches galore. Moreover, on the first morning, when trying to stop a boundary, Denis fell awkwardly into the fence and fractured the third finger in his left hand. Apart from going in twice at the bottom end of the order he took no further part in the match. Australia won by an innings and 154 runs with more than a day to spare.

England's bowling analysis made painful reading: Bedser, who was still not wholly fit after a debilitating attack of shingles, one for 131; Statham two for 123; Tyson one for 160; Bailey three for 140. Denis's views as senior professional had been sought before the match began, and he accepts his share of the blame for a gamble that went horribly wrong.

England were bowled out for 190 and 257. Hutton, who had begun his tour in prime form, failed twice. Predictably enough, when the going was tough in the first innings, Bailey got 88, his best score against Australia, in an innings lasting more than four hours. When Denis came in last, to bat with one hand, Bailey hit out and was bowled, virtually surrendering his wicket so that his partner should not be long exposed to further troubles. Denis was 2 not out. In England's second innings Edrich also made 88, by a long way the most imposing score in his four Test matches that series. For Denis to bat a second time, in a hopeless cause, seemed akin to playing with fire. On this occasion he went in at number 10, Benaud having him caught behind for nought.

He was to miss four weeks of the action, including the second Test match which took place in Sydney shortly before Christmas. He has recorded in one of his own books how Len Hutton was persuaded to play in it only at the eleventh hour. No doubt the mental pressure felt by the captain explained how Alec Bedser discovered that he had been left out of the side by observing the sad fact on the team sheet. Yet Hutton's courageous and difficult decision to drop England's faithful warhorse was amply justified by events. Statham and Tyson (who had now been persuaded to operate off a shorter run) twice ripped out Australia for a victory, by 38 runs, that did wonders for English morale and squared the series at one-all.

The reduction in Tyson's run-up did nothing to reduce his awesome speed. Tom Graveney swears that he stood forty yards back in the slips. He has never seen such pace. 'In the second innings, Neil Harvey, who got a magnificent 92 not out, looked to be the only Australian able to

A little bowling practice at Eton College before their match with Forty Club in 1956. This was Denis's first game of cricket after another operation involving the removal of a knee cap

Denis, Bill Edrich and (on the right) Reg Simpson with stars of an ice show in Adelaide during the successful tour of Australia in 1954/55

Opposite left: *With Sir Leonard Hutton at a party marking Denis's retirement from full-time cricket at the end of the 1957 season*

Opposite right: *And together again, at a charity match in Bickley, Kent, in 1958 – with this biographer happily bringing up the rear*

Opposite below: *The Courage Old England XI practising in Aldwych in May 1981. Left to right: Dick Richardson, John Edrich, Godfrey Evans, Denis, Fred Titmus and Fred Trueman*

Above: *With John Carlisle MP and Bill Edrich at the MCC special general meeting called in 1983 to debate whether the club should send a touring side to South Africa*

Right: *Denis and Christine. They were married in 1975*

Above left: *Three score years and ten: a photograph taken at the Nursery End at Lord's on his 70th birthday. The stance is more open than the one pictured in his 'teens. But note the grip on the bat: hands together, close to the top of the handle*

Above right: *Another 70th birthday picture at Lord's. Denis is holding a figurine of himself in the 'cricket in miniature' series*

Left: *In reflective mood at the Guildhall when MCC celebrated their Bicentenary in 1987*

lay a bat on him.' England scored 154 and 296. Peter May, 104, and Colin Cowdrey, 54, shared in an Oxbridge partnership of rare quality. Australia totalled 228 and 184, Tyson, with the wind, taking six for 85 and finishing the match, which was over on the penultimate day, with a haul of ten wickets.

Making his return to the side in a two day game at Newcastle at the end of December, Denis signalled his well-being with a good 60. He was back in the England XI for the third Test match, played in Melbourne at the New Year on an unpredictable pitch which, it was proved, had been watered on the rest day. The local cricket authorities subsequently denied it. Whatever the truth of the matter, Australia were no better able to deal with Statham and Tyson in a second relatively low-scoring contest.

England made 191 (Cowdrey 102) and 279 (May 91), Australia 231 and 111 to lose by 128 runs, yet again with a day in hand. In Australia's first innings Statham took five for 60, and Tyson two for 68. In their second innings, *Wisden* reports Tyson as having blazed through the opposition like a bush fire. 'Sheer speed through the air coupled with the chance of a shooter at any moment left the Australian batsmen nonplussed.' The last eight wickets crashed down for 36 runs, Tyson capturing six of them for just 16 and Statham getting the others. The 'typhoon' walked off with figures of seven for 27. The catch with which Evans dismissed Harvey off his bowling is still remembered.

Denis's personal share in this rousing success was modest. In the first innings he was taken in the gully for 4 when trying to fend down an unpleasant rising ball from Miller, and in his second, when still feeling pain from the bruise, he got to 23 before Ron Archer had him caught by the wicket keeper down the leg side. He had little time to observe Cowdrey's masterful hundred at close quarters. If one adds his scores in the present Test series to date to those he endured on his previous visit to Australia, it makes for unhappy reading. He was clearly overdue for a turn in his luck.

A 46 against a Combined XI in Hobart was followed by a lordly 50 against Tasmania at Launceston and another half-century against a South Australian Country XI. He then, in the return game against South Australia, made 182 in four and three-quarter hours, his first hundred for two months and the highest MCC score of the tour. But the big score he was looking for against Australia was denied him in the fourth Test in Adelaide.

He got a useful 44 in the first innings, Miller having him lbw with an inswinger, and a more than handy 34 not out in the second after England, in final pursuit of 94, had suffered some nasty shocks at the hands of the same bowler. The great all-rounder disposed of Edrich, Hutton and Cowdrey in the course of twenty balls. That left England on 18 for three, at which point their captain is said to have observed in the dressing room. 'Those Australian boogers have done us again.' 'Hang on,' Denis said, picking up his bat and going out to the middle at number 5, 'We only want 94.'

Miller was not done with yet. England's total was 49 when he ended May's innings of 26 with a superlative catch in the covers, whereupon the trusty Bailey joined Compton and the pair of them all but saw their side home. Four runs were still needed when Bailey was leg before to Bill Johnston. Godfrey Evans then sallied forth to make the winning hit. Denis carried out his bat for 34, and England had recorded, by five wickets, their third successive victory. It gave them their first success in a Test rubber in Australia since the Bodyline tour of 1932/33, and the Ashes were retained.

This Test match in Adelaide, played throughout in temperatures around the hundred mark, was the only one of the series in which both sides got past 300. It was a good toss for Australia to win but England, with 341, took a first innings lead of 18, whereupon Tyson, Statham and Appleyard bowled out the opposition a second time for 111. Tyson with six wickets in the match brought his tally in three successive Test matches to 25. But it was Appleyard, brought on very early by Hutton to exploit patches worn by the bowlers' footholds, who on this occasion made the most critical breakthrough. On the fourth evening he accounted for Arthur Morris, Jim Burke and Neil Harvey for 6 runs in as many overs.

On the last morning Hutton reverted to an all-out pace attack, Statham and Tyson yet again reigning supreme in an unbroken spell of an hour and a half during which they shared six wickets and Australia managed just another 34 runs. For the fourth time in the series there was to be no need of a sixth day's play.

This was the Test in which Hutton in the first innings made 80, by some way his best effort of the series. Cowdrey followed that with 79, during the course of which Denis, then sharing a promising partnership for the fourth wicket, said to him. 'Davo [Alan Davidson] can't have more than one or two overs left. After that no one's going to get us out on this wicket.' Miller had other ideas.

England called all the shots during an abbreviated fifth Test match, in Sydney. It could not start until after lunch on the fourth day, some incessantly heavy rains having inundated the Hunter Valley. Put in to bat, England declared at 371 for seven, bowled out Australia for 221 and then in the follow-on had them, when time expired, on the rack at 118 for six. Johnny Wardle had three of those to add to his five for 79 in the first innings.

In his last Test match against Australia, and as things turned out, the last of his career, Len Hutton was out for 6. But Tom Graveney, who went in first with him, stroked his elegant way to a lovely 111, May weighed in with 79, Denis got 84 and Bailey 72. Bailey gave Lindwall his hundredth England Test wicket when the acceleration was imminent. In his last game for England in Melbourne four years later, he was to collect a pair from the same bowler. Denis's 84 was not his greatest Test innings. Alan Ross in *Australia '55* thought very little of the progress made by Compton and Bailey when on the second morning, from an overnight score of 196 for four, they managed to add only 51 in two hours. In due course, however, England were able to enforce the follow-on by one run.

Denis, twice not out in seven innings, finished the series with 191 runs at an average of 38.20, no mean effort after what had happened to him in Brisbane. Len Hutton was well down the list, scoring 220 at 24.44 from two innings more. In all first-class matches Compton and Hutton still headed the averages. But the old guard, as Alan Ross observed, had made way for the younger brigade. England no longer leant so heavily on the triumvirate of Hutton, Compton and Bedser, although Bailey, at 31, was still going strongly. May, Cowdrey, Statham and Tyson were all 25 or less.

His knee by now a constant problem, Denis did not go on to New Zealand for the last leg of the tour. Instead, he flew to South Africa to join his wife, Valerie, and enjoyed, as the hero he has always been in that country, a rapturous welcome at Johannesburg airport. He had had time, before leaving Australia, to organize an invitation, along with a few of his colleagues, to a barbecue on Sydney Harbour beach. The only snag, as Frank Tyson recalls, was that the party had taken place the evening before.

1955: Still Rising to the Big Occasion

O**N ACCOUNT OF TEST CALLS** and persistent knee problems – which came to a head at the end of the series against South Africa – Denis in 1955 experienced his least productive season for Middlesex since he had arrived so excitingly on the first-class scene nineteen years before. The county missed his services for seventeen of their games, and in the twenty innings he played for them he reached 50 on only four occasions and finished the championship season with the very modest return of 590 runs at 31.05. Since a decline in his contribution was accompanied by one from his captain that was even more marked, Bill Edrich in his full championship programme managing 1,296 at 26.44, it was not surprising that Middlesex's progress was inconsistent. It was largely thanks to the bowling of Fred Titmus and Alan Moss, staunchly supported by Jack Young and J. J. Warr, that they managed to finish fifth.

For Denis, retaining his ability to rise to important occasions, the Test series, in which he played a full part, produced far happier results. His tally of 492 runs at 54.66 was certainly nothing to feel ashamed about. Only his captain, May, did better.

In 1955 Denis was not the only distinguished England batsman to experience physical problems. In his third game of the season, for MCC against the South Africans, his captain, Len Hutton, who was to be appointed to lead England throughout the Test series, was seized by an attack of lumbago at the start of his first innings and took no further part. A fortnight later Hutton had to withdraw from the first Test, May taking over as the England captain. The career of a great batsman was drawing to its end.

In that encounter at Lord's Denis made 25 and 20 – running himself out in the second innings. Jack Cheetham's Springboks got their tails up and won by 93 runs. In their next match Middlesex ran into a sticky dog of a pitch at Bristol. 'Bomber' Wells, who was playing for Gloucestershire, recalls that although the ball was turning square for the left-hander, Sam Cook, Denis time and again made room to hit him where he pleased through the covers. He scored 44. 'Bomber' thought it the best innings he had ever seen.

After a performance such as that something rather special seemed to be on the cards, and so it proved. Twenty thousand spectators gathered at Lord's on Whit Monday, after the first day's play was lost to rain, to witness Middlesex playing Sussex in a joint benefit match for Harry Sharp and Alec Thompson. By lunch, Middlesex had subsided to 54 for five, but an important, perhaps vital, wicket had yet to fall. I am now obliged to Alan Moss for details of the conversation that ensued. 'Don't muck about, Compo,' said Sharp, who was looking distinctly worried. 'Don't worry,' Compo replied. 'I'll get you a hundred. How do you want them? In two's or four's?'

There followed, as *Wisden* faithfully records, 'a superb innings by Denis Compton that transcended all else'. The bare details speak for themselves; 50 out of 64, 100 out of 135, 150 (c Suttle b Marlar) out of 195. The next highest score in a total of 206 was 13 by J. J. Warr. An astounding effort which augured well for Denis and England in the Test series shortly to begin at Trent Bridge. It was to be an exciting one in a lovely summer.

The South Africans had arrived in England sustained by a memory of their splendid performance in Australia in 1952/53, when they came from behind in the final Test match to draw the series at two-all. But the result at Trent Bridge, England winning by an innings and 5 runs, left them needing their proven powers of recovery.

It was not a dramatic contest. Pinned down by negative bowling, which was supported by electric fielding, Denis needed an hour and forty minutes to contribute 27 towards England's innings of 334 before Neil Adcock had him lbw. When South Africa batted, their little opening batsman, Jackie McGlew, twice put up the shutters to make 68 and 51 in more than nine hours of adhesive resistance. When they followed on, Frank Tyson, whose pace remained fearful then, blasted them out with six for 28.

In the second Test, at Lord's, England won again, this time by 71 runs, to take an apparently firm grip on the rubber. It was a much better game of cricket, played on a fast pitch which was green enough on the first morning to offer Adcock and Peter Heine some disconcerting bounce. Denis always had the healthiest respect for this pair of fast bowlers. Heine had him caught for 20, off a ball that flew from just short of a length. England made a total of 133. It had been a useful toss for Jack Cheetham to lose.

South Africa then took a substantial first innings lead of 171 with Roy McLean making a brilliant 142, out of 196 added while he was in,

141

in only three and a half hours. England paid dearly for dropped catches. But thanks mainly to Tom Graveney (60) Peter May (112) and Denis (69) they then made 353 in their second innings and South Africa, needing 183 to level the series, were all out for 111. Bowling unchanged for almost four hours, Brian Statham did magnificently to return figures of seven for 39, the most shining of this great-hearted cricketer's career so far.

In the course of his 69, an innings revealing him almost at his best, Denis became only the fifth batsman in Test match history to pass the milestone of 5,000 runs. Walter Hammond, Sir Donald Bradman, Len Hutton and Sir John Berry Hobbs were then the only names standing above him in the hall of fame.

Colin Cowdrey recalls that when he received his official invitation to play in the third Test at Old Trafford in 1955, there was a note from Gubby Allen, chairman of selectors, which said, 'Please note that the 3 p.m. meeting for net practice on the Wednesday does not mean 3.10.' Everyone knew whom the chairman was getting at, and Colin Cowdrey subsequently had the invitation framed. But at Old Trafford on the eve of the match there was no sign of Denis at 3 o'clock, nor 4, nor even 5, when England's practice was concluded. The absentee, looking immaculate but somewhat sheepish, eventually turned up at the team's hotel in Lymm at around 8 p.m. The chairman, not best pleased to say the least, demanded an explanation.

It appeared that on the Tuesday, his 50 in 34 minutes having helped to polish off Worcestershire by lunchtime, Denis decided to pop down from Worcester to Middleton-on-Sea in Sussex where his wife and family were on holiday. From there, next morning, he intended to drive home to collect his gear in Buckinghamshire, and go from there to Manchester. But, alas, by the time he got home he was far enough behind schedule to beseech a friend who owned his own aeroplane to fly him northwards. This explains how, about two hours before he was due in the nets, his presence in the saloon bar at the Bull in Gerrards Cross occasioned some knowing amusement amongst those who knew the cricketing form.

Unfortunately, the twin-seater aircraft was so small that Denis had to leave his cricket bag behind and took with him, apart from his clothes in which he sat, one white shirt, one pair of flannels, one pair of boots, one England sweater and one toothbrush. Even more unfortunately, the aircraft for some reason had to divert from Manchester to Derby, from where Denis took an expensive taxi ride.

Gubby Allen's wrath was assuaged, but on pain of death Denis was required to present himself for nets at 9 a.m. on the morning of the match. In due course England won the toss and Denis, with a bat borrowed from Fred Titmus, who had recently made his Test debut at Lord's, went in fourth at 22 for two. Tom Graveney and Don Kenyon had already departed for 0 and 5 respectively, and South Africa's opening bowlers were extracting a lot of unpleasant bounce. But the new batsman, after a shaky start, battled away for five and a half hours to make 158.

'He fought magnificently,' Cowdrey remembers. But he thinks that the 71 Denis made in the second innings was arguably the best he ever saw him play. 'Tayfield pitched five successive balls on a sixpence, and Compo dispatched each one to various parts of the boundary.' Neil Adcock says he could never set a field to Denis at his best. 'He was so difficult to bowl at because of his facility to place the ball, and he had a fantastic ability to play it late. But I always felt he gave you a bit of a chance.'

Twenty-three years later, Cowdrey was to make one of the speeches when Middlesex and the Beecham Group celebrated Denis's 70th birthday. 'Tell you what,' he recalled him saying at Old Trafford, 'if only I'd arrived in time for practice . . .'

A resurgent South Africa scored 521 for eight declared in their first innings, with McGlew, Johnny Waite and Paul Winslow all making hundreds and England spilling some more catches. Winslow obviously liked Old Trafford. Against Lancashire he had previously struck 40 off eight successive balls. He now smote three sixes and thirteen fours in an innings of 108.

Although Peter May got yet another hundred, his partnership with Denis producing some sparkling cricket, South Africa's final target of 145 in two and a quarter hours proved to be just within their grasp in the time available. Tension in the Springbok dressing room was so extreme that Heine (no.10) and Adcock (no.11) got their pads on when the fourth wicket went down at 112. South Africa got home by three wickets with nine balls left.

There was another dazzling, shorter innings of 50 by McLean, and McGlew got a brisk 48 to add to the 104 not out he made in the first innings. The little man had better luck than at Lord's where he got an ignominious pair, Statham dismissing him twice in three balls. The Old Trafford Test was Alec Bedser's last for England. One of the all-time great medium-fast bowlers retired with what was then a world record of 236 wickets.

Returning to Lord's for his county's game against Yorkshire, Denis kept himself in trim with 84 in an hour and a half, but was bowled by Freddie Trueman in his second innings when failing to trouble the scorers. He then journeyed to Headingley for the fourth Test match.

England looked to have the match and series wrapped up after South Africa, winning the toss for the only time in the rubber, were bowled out by Statham and Peter Loader for 171. But in spite of Adcock having to retire with a nasty foot injury after bowling only four overs, the England batting lost its way on a bland pitch against some splendid bowling from Heine, Goddard and Tayfield. Denis got top score of 61, Peter May made 47, and England were held to a first innings lead of just 20. Everyone found Goddard, left-arm medium over the wicket, extremely hard to get away. Yet his figures of 25–12–39–2 were not nearly as impressive as those he returned in the second innings.

Reprieved by England's inadequate batting, South Africa now took command with a second innings of exactly 500 with McGlew and Russell Endean both making centuries. That left England with a highly improbable target of 481 and South Africa's bowlers plenty of time to bowl them out. It was no surprise when England succumbed, shortly before tea on the final day, by 224 runs.

Their captain Peter May, then at the peak of his powers, made 97. Denis got 26 before he was caught behind off Goddard, who bowled unchanged from first to last that final day for the quite remarkable analysis of 62–37–69–5. On any other day, that of Tayfield – 47.1–15–94–5 – would have attracted the main spotlight. It was a fine victory for South Africa, who had now squared the series after being two down.

Colin Cowdrey and Godfrey Evans were unfit for the final Test. England brought in Jack Ikin, Brian Close, Willie Watson and Dick Spooner (to keep wicket) on the theory that four left-handed batsmen would be a counter to Goddard – although, of course, Hugh Tayfield, as an off-spinner, might prefer their presence. Fourth innings totals at The Oval were not substantial at that time, so Jack Cheetham's feelings on losing the toss yet again can be imagined. England won a low-scoring contest, and with it the rubber, by 92 runs on the fourth day, Jim Laker and Tony Lock taking fifteen of the eighteen South African wickets that fell to bowlers.

Denis got 30 in a first innings of 151 but his knee was playing up badly and by the time he batted again it was causing him considerable pain. In spite of this he stuck it out for two and a quarter hours, making 30 again, and helping his skipper to improve on England's first innings lead of 39. Their final total was 204, which was more than enough. May's 89 not out was crucially important. So indeed was Tayfield's contribution to South Africa's attack. By stumps on the third day, having bowled without relief for five hours, he had sent down 52 overs for 54 runs and four wickets, figures thought by *Wisden* to be without parallel in Test cricket.

It was no surprise that the shackles imposed upon Denis by a serious recurrence of his knee problem limited the quality of his end-of-season performances. In the fifteen innings – ten of them for Middlesex – he played following his 61 in the Headingley Test match his highest score was 34. It had to be a matter of keeping going, mostly in a very low gear.

By the end of the season the knee was so swollen and painful that his surgeons, Bill Tucker and Osmond Clarke, decided that if he was to play again his only chance lay in having his kneecap removed. A successful operation was performed in University College Hospital where, sadly, Denis's old Arsenal manager, Tom Whittaker, lay dying in a nearby ward.

The 1955 summer was the last for Denis's great England contemporary Len Hutton, upon whom a knighthood was conferred in the Birthday Honours of 1956. How many runs, how many hundreds, might he and Denis have made but for their physical afflictions or the years lost to the war?

1956: 94 In Only Test *v* Australia

DENIS'S NEW SEASON did not in fact begin until the end of June, by which time England had played two Test matches against their oldest of cricketing enemies in defence of the Ashes. By then, England found themselves one down.

Shortly after the England party had returned home from the New Zealand leg of their previous tour, Australia set off under Ian Johnson for the Caribbean, where they defeated the West Indies comprehensively by three matches to none. This was in spite of the fact that Clyde Walcott set new records, with five hundreds in the Test series, including two in the same match twice. Australia's bowling – notably that of Ray Lindwall, Keith Miller, Ron Archer and Richie Benaud – was greatly superior. On their home pitches Sonny Ramadhin and Alfred Valentine could not recapture the magic that had mesmerized England in 1950. Australia notched up totals of 515 for nine declared, 600 likewise, 668 and 758 for eight declared. In that last innings five batsmen made hundreds: Colin McDonald, Neil Harvey (204), Miller, Archer and Benaud, who reached three figures in seventy-eight minutes.

All of these century makers were leading figures in the Australian touring team which found the going distinctly more difficult in England in 1956. It had the misfortune to run into one of our wettest and most miserable summers, and conditions almost tailor-made for Messrs Laker and Lock.

Denis had still not picked up a bat for eight months when in mid-May Jim Laker startled the Australians – and the whole cricket world – by taking all ten of their first innings wickets when they played Surrey at The Oval. Bowling unchanged for four and a quarter hours on a bone dry pitch he achieved figures of 46–18–88–10. The ball turned less readily for Ian Johnson. And it is worth recalling, in the light of what was to happen in the Old Trafford Test, that Tony Lock, bowling from the less responsive Vauxhall end, had a return of 33–12–100–0.

Lock duly came into his own with seven for 49 in the second innings, and Surrey romped home by ten wickets to become the first county to beat an Australian touring side since 1912. (Gloucestershire had played a nail-biting tie against Bill Woodfull's side in 1930.) By the time the Test series ended, Australia could justly bemoan their luck about losing four tosses out of five. They had no such cause for complaint in their game against Surrey.

England's most distinguished absentee was thinking about trying out his knee in a one-day game or two when the first Test, at Trent Bridge, was drawn after more than twelve hours' play had been lost to rain. Winning the toss and enjoying the best of the batting conditions in both of their innings, England declared twice but ran out of time when Australia, left four hours to get 258, were content to finish on 120 for three. They experienced trouble in the first innings against Laker (six wickets overall) and Lock (four), but the draw was by no means a moral victory for England. In their first innings Alan Davidson, who was to become one of the great left-arm swing bowlers, suffered a severe ankle injury which kept him out of the next three Tests, and Ray Lindwall, now in his 35th year, pulled up lame with a recurrence of an old thigh injury.

Lindwall was obliged to miss the second Test at Lord's. In this match, Ian Johnson got the toss right for the only time and Australia won the match, squarely enough, by 185 runs. The absence of his sparring partner inspired Keith Miller, then 36, to take five wickets twice. He was to finish the series at the head of Australia's bowling, with 21 wickets in all. Lindwall was to end it with just seven. Never, I think, completely fit, he had lost some of the old zip though nothing of the old guile or his capacity to swing a new ball. The famous pair of fast bowlers found hard, fast pitches very hard to come by that summer.

At this point I return from the story of the 1956 series to concentrate on my main subject. Denis was about to play his first match of the season for Middlesex, against Lancashire at Lord's. Alan Moss, another fast bowler who broke down in the Trent Bridge Test match, could not play against Lancashire but he was down at the Nursery end when Denis made a rare appearance for net practice on the first morning of the game. 'Everything he stood in was probably begged, borrowed or stolen,' Moss recalls. 'The pitch was wet, a bloody puddin'. He looked hardly able to move, so the bowlers gave him some dollies at first. Then they quickened up to the full treatment. After a quarter of an hour there wasn't a mark on or even close to the edge of his bat. There was just one solid dark circle in the middle.'

Not that this impressive performance did Denis much good when his turn came to bat: he made only 4 and 1. However, the golden touch was still there in other ways. On that first day, in front of 17,000 spectators, he caught three of the first four Lancashire batsmen at slip and, coming on as fourth change bowler, took Alan Wharton's wicket with his fifth ball. This was the first occasion that Peter Parfitt, who made his debut for the county that season, heard Denis referred to as 'Gold'. But 'Gold', who had done it yet again, found a day in the field to be extremely taxing. He finished it limping and weary.

Denis did not feel in shape to play in his county's next encounter, against Essex. But he rejoined the side for the following fixture, against Somerset at Glastonbury, with a highly encouraging effort. It was Maurice Tremlett's benefit match, and Denis declared that he would make a hundred for him. This was one of only three occasions when, as John Warr remembers, he heard Denis boast. Back in 1954, Denis had said he would get one for brother Les's benefit, but he ran out of time and partners, as well as running out his brother. In the following summer he predicted the same for the joint benefit of Harry Sharp and Alec Thompson, and duly reached his target. Peter Parfitt recollects the 110 that Denis made for Tremlett.

'It was a marled works ground wicket, very, very slow, and a turner. He went up the track on one decent knee against Colin McCool and though he couldn't always quite get there he still thrust him away through the covers. He batted magnificently. It was the only time I can truthfully say that I'd seen genius at work.' It goes without saying that this innings did wonders for Denis's confidence. But it is time to take up the story of the Test series again.

England were now one down, with three to play. Announcing the side for the Headingley Test the selectors dropped a sizeable stone in the pond by bringing in one of their own number, Cyril Washbrook, in place of Tom Graveney. Washbrook, then 41 but still in fine fettle for Lancashire, had played his last Test match in New Zealand at the end of the MCC's Australasian tour in 1950/51.

It was a substantial gamble on the part of the selectors and, goodness knows, it came desperately close to failure when Ron Archer, who had ripped out the first three England wickets for 17, soon afterwards must have been within a whisker of having Washbrook lbw on the back foot. Washbrook went on to make 98, his third-wicket partnership of 187 with Peter May (101) giving England control of the game. They totalled 325, and just what a good toss it had been to win was revealed as Laker and Lock, on a turning pitch more and more to their liking, bowled out Australia for 143 and 140. Laker had match figures of eleven for 113, Lock seven for 81. England levelled the series at one-all with a victory by an innings and 42 runs.

Back now to Denis, currently engaged with Middlesex at Gloucester, where he made a lively 47. During this game Tom Graveney told him that he had been having some trouble with his bats, whereupon Denis lent him his. It suited Tom a treat, for he made a resounding 156 in his second innings. 'You keep it, old boy,' said Denis, to whom all forms of willow seemed more or less to come alike.

He was clearly ready now to represent the Players again in the 150th anniversary of their traditional match against the Gentlemen. Though making only a modest 25, in little more than half an hour, he made problems look simple while others laboured. His next game was for Middlesex against the Australians at Lord's.

Put in the baldest terms, he made 50, out of 62, in a shade over an hour and a quarter, and 61 altogether. I quote now from what I wrote in *The Fight for the Ashes 1956*: 'We sat back and marvelled at an innings which, considering all the circumstances, was perhaps the most brilliant I saw all season. And I saw nothing finer all summer than the piece of fielding which ended it. Compton . . . drove Benaud very hard towards the gap between mid-off and extra cover. It looked a certain four; I think Compton thought it was as he ambled up the wicket. But Harvey swooped like lightning from extra, picked up one-handed and with a wonderful return threw down the wicket at the bowler's end. In his athletic prime Compton would not have stood a chance; nor now, if he had been jet-propelled.' Richie Benaud has lately brought me up-to-date with another detail about this dismissal. 'Oh! Christ,' Denis said, the moment of awful truth revealed. 'It's Harvey!'

After this rousing display Denis was able to take a week off, and enjoyed watching television pictures of the remarkable fourth Test match at Old Trafford. Jim Laker's astonishing, record-breaking feat of taking nineteen wickets for 90 runs (nine for 37, ten for 53) has been so well chronicled that I am tempted merely to record the fact that England won by an innings and 170 runs and thus made sure of retaining the Ashes. But it remains to be stressed that it was another excellent toss for England to win and that the selectors came up trumps with their second inspired choice of the series, the Rev. David Sheppard making 113. From what he observed on television Denis thought the Australians were fully entitled to complain about the Old Trafford pitch – and that at Headingley as well.

In the first two weeks of August, Denis got a fifty against Hampshire and then, following a run of low scores, 101 against Kent at Lord's. 'A sparkling innings,' *Wisden* records, 'occupying three hours and ten minutes, and including sixteen fours.' By his own standards, the time he took for it was somewhat above par for the course.

All of the innings played by Denis at Lord's since his return to the first-class scene had been watched by Gubby Allen, chairman of England's selectors. With the fifth Test only six days away, and the announcement of their final side all but due, the chairman asked Denis if he felt ready to play at The Oval. He added that the captain, Peter May, wanted him in the side. Denis had already thought hard about his answer to such a question. 'Yes,' he said. 'And if I fail, I'll call it a day.' So the name of D. C. S. Compton was marked in and on the eve of the match, by way of bolstering his confidence, the public was also advised that he would be one of those players touring South Africa in the winter.

England, having won the toss yet again, were 66 for three when, to another stirring ovation, Denis walked out to the middle to join his captain. There was a pat on the head, and the conventional welcome from Keith Miller who could not have been more pleased to see his old friend and adversary back in action. On a greenish pitch Miller had already accounted for Peter Richardson and David Sheppard. Colin Cowdrey had succumbed, for nought, to a superb outswinger from Ray Lindwall.

Sedately getting his bearings, and needing fifteen minutes to get off the mark, Denis from the start of his innings gave his legions of supporters very little cause for concern. Suffice it to say that he and May carried the England total to 222, his share of a partnership of 156 being 94, before a leg-glance off Ron Archer's bowling was swallowed up by Alan Davidson, moving swiftly to his left at backward short leg. He had been put down once, on 69, when Archer at slip missed a sharpish chance off Miller who, without much luck but with relentless zeal, was the cornerstone of Australia's attack.

Sir Donald Bradman, reporting the series for the *Daily Mail*, thought Denis had played the best innings in the series. It certainly completed an inspired piece of English selection. The four selectors (joined of course by the captain) were G. O. Allen (chairman), Leslie Ames, Cyril Washbrook and Wilfred Wooller.

Having collapsed to a total of 247 all out after Denis's departure, with May remaining undefeated on 93, England took a first innings lead of 45. But the fourth day was lost to rain and England did not have time enough to force another victory. May (37) and Denis (35) were together again, undefeated, when the captain declared their second innings closed at 182 for three. May had averaged 90 in the series.

Australia, 227 in arrears, with two hours left to play out time, were still due for some nasty shocks. Brian Statham, bowling his first and only over of the innings, had Colin McDonald lbw to his second ball. Lock bowled the second over, Laker the third. In no time Australia were five for three wickets. But Miller hung in there and when bad light ended the match on a gloomy, draughty evening the score was 27 for five.

Miller could have wished to end his Test career against England in happier circumstances. Laker finished with three for 8 off 18 overs, 14 of them maidens, to bring his tally in the series to an astonishing 46 wickets at an average of 9.60. Of the 132 wickets he took that season in all first-class matches, 58 were those of the Australian touring side.

Denis played in just eleven first-class matches in 1956, eight of them for Middlesex who finished fifth in the county championship. Significantly enough, the captain, Edrich, topped their batting with 1,427 runs at a modest 32.43, and Denis came next with 405 at 31.15.

1956/57: Bowing Out For England

WHEN PETER MAY led his MCC side to South Africa in 1956/57 England were arguably the strongest team in world cricket. At that time they had not lost a Test series since their defeat in Australia in 1950/51, and their success was to continue, beyond Denis's international span, until the winter of 1958/59 when, again under the captaincy of May, a team bristling with all-round talent bit the dust 4–0 in Australia. It would be truer, perhaps, to record that many of us thought they were 'thrown out' by Meckiff and Rorke. However, there was nothing wrong with the bowling actions of Davidson or Benaud, the new Australian skipper, both of whom played a full part in England's eclipse. But that is another story.

In South Africa in 1956/57 the England batting for the first three Test matches was led by Peter Richardson, Trevor Bailey (promoted to open), Denis Compton, Peter May, Colin Cowdrey and Doug. Insole, who was to top the averages. If that seemed a more than adequate line-up, the bowling resources at May's command looked even more impressive: Brian Statham, Frank Tyson, Bailey, Peter Loader, Johnny Wardle, Jim Laker and Tony Lock, who played only in the fifth Test, when Wardle was injured.

It turned out to be a dour, unspectacular series, on slow or unreliable pitches. An overall run rate of only 30 per 100 balls tells its own story. But it was made memorable in the end by South Africa coming back from two-down to square it with victories in the last two matches.

In such conditions it was not surprising that both sides bowled more effectively than they batted. No batsman averaged 40 or more in the Tests; bowlers dominated, none more so than Wardle and Bailey for England and Hugh Tayfield, Neil Adcock and Trevor Goddard for the home side. The versatile Wardle, for the most part concentrating on his left-handed off-breaks and wrong 'uns, took 26 wickets in the Test series at the remarkable average of 13.80 – though Bailey with 19 wickets had marginally better figures – and 105 in all the 22 games played on a long, demanding and tiring tour. This must remain the outstanding post-war overseas performance by an England spin bowler.

'Toey' Tayfield's off-breaks and 'floaters', pitched to an unyielding length, were even more successful. Taking eight wickets in England's second innings during the third Test – which was drawn, to signal

South Africa's recovery – and nine in the corresponding one of the fourth, he finished with a haul of 37 wickets at 17.18.

Denis, no longer able to get down the pitch to him, suffered agonies of frustration, as he did when facing the nagging medium pace of the left-handed Goddard, whose attack, directed on or just outside the leg stump to a restrictive on-side field, had tied him down in England in 1955. In his heyday Denis would surely have gone down the track to both of these bowlers; now he could not even snatch the quick singles. It was as if a dead weight kept him shackled to the crease.

He struggled to make 242 runs in the series, top score 64, at an average of 24.20. More remarkably, his captain finished it two places lower with 153 runs, top score 61, and an average of 15.30, in spite of a glorious start to the tour which had brought him five hundreds – one of them a doubleton – in six first-class matches. In the other fixtures Peter May went on doing much as he pleased but his run of low scores in the Test series, some of them due to brilliant catching, evoked echoes of Denis's miserable sequence in Australia in 1950/51. From that experience Denis knew all about the pressures that are built up by continuing failure.

After achieving nothing of note in the opening two first-class games Denis found himself, after MCC had thrashed Orange Free State by an innings, with a week of leisure. If this should surprise tourists exposed to today's schedules, a story put about by Peter Parfitt, though it may owe something to poetic licence, may carry more credence.

That relentless teller of tales holds that Denis and Peter Richardson left the party, with full approval of captain Peter May and manager Freddie Brown, to spend time in Johannesburg before rejoining the side for two matches against Rhodesia, in Bulawayo and Salisbury. It appears that when the pair of them went their separate ways at Johannesburg airport, Richardson was unwise enough to leave onward ticketing arrangements to his partner. In due course the pair were reunited, and flew to Salisbury where the following conversation is alleged to have taken place in an hotel:

Manager: 'I'm delighted to welcome you, gentlemen, but aren't you rather early for the game?'

Compton (looking smug): 'I always like to be on time. Where are the rest of the lads?'

Manager: 'Well, I should think they're in Bulawayo because the first game is being played there.'

This is, I think, too good to leave out. Were I to ask Denis to

153

corroborate the essential facts, he might well deny them before putting the matter in the hands of his solicitor.

Shortly afterwards Denis was reviving memories of the buoyant times with 72 against Transvaal and a dazzling 71 not out against weaker opposition, North-Eastern Transvaal. In the first of these games Statham achieved a hat-trick, all clean bowled.

So to the start of the series, and the first Test played over Christmas on the new Wanderers ground in Johannesburg. After bowling out South Africa for 72 in their second innings (Bailey five for 20), England won convincingly by 131 runs. It had been a good toss to win on a difficult pitch. In 488 minutes Richardson ground out what was then the slowest hundred in Test match history.

For Denis, alas, his knee was troubling him once more. He made 5 and 32, at one stage adding just 15 in almost two hours before he departed, caught and bowled by Tayfield. Although the bowler was apparently the only player on the field who thought the ball had carried, Denis walked at once. Doug Insole, who was in with him at the time, suggested that he should wait for the umpire's verdict. Denis kept on going.

In the second Test in Cape Town in the new year, England's captain declined to enforce the follow-on and South Africa, routed yet again for 72 in their second innings, were beaten even more conclusively by 312 runs. Denis grafted away for his best scores in the series, 58 and 64, but it was awfully hard work. Wardle enjoyed match figures of twelve for 89.

In his next two provincial games Denis got his two hundreds of the tour, 101 against Natal and 131 against Transvaal. E. W. Swanton in *Report from South Africa 1956/57* wrote that after his century Denis produced an astonishing display of strokes. In between these encounters came the third Test in Durban which John Woodcock, for so long cricket correspondent of *The Times*, still asserts England would have won had their captain not taken Wardle off in South Africa's second innings. If, as I suspect, he was right, England would have wrapped up the series. As it was, South Africa hung out for a draw.

In his first innings Denis, seeking to glance Peter Heine, was bowled behind his legs for 16. In his second, he struck a long hop from Tayfield straight at one of the two forward short-legs and was out for 3 runs more.

The Springboks, fielding like demons, had the bit between their teeth now. In Johannesburg again, having won the toss for the first time in the series, they gained an exciting victory by 17 runs. In a marathon bowling performance spread over more than five hours, Tayfield captured nine wickets in England's second innings for 113 runs.

Tayfield's influence on the series was profound. In his first innings Denis got 42, at one stage playing sixty-seven balls from Tayfield without making a run and enduring a scoreless period of almost an hour. In two hours before tea he slaved to make just 13. The late Ron Roberts, respected journalist and touring entrepreneur, recorded that his timing was all awry. 'It was nothing short of a nightmare.' When Denis went in a second time he was yet again pinioned by Tayfield before edging him to slip. He had managed one single.

The toss at Port Elizabeth, won by South Africa, was crucial since the pitch prepared for the fifth Test match on a new strip was quite unsuitable for a match of good cricket. John Woodcock thought it had the lowest bounce of any he had ever seen. Shooters abounded. It was not good policy to be on the back foot. In a low-scoring encounter South Africa's first innings of 164 was the highest total by either side. Although Adcock and Heine had prospered in the early stages it was Tayfield (six for 78) who finally wrapped up the South African victory by 58 runs.

In England's first innings Adcock had Richardson lbw to the sixth ball of the second over after he thought he had had him trapped by the first. The last one in an eight-ball over, an inswinger, accounted for Denis, also for no score. So to his second effort, and a reflection by E. W. Swanton that 'after all the brilliant innings he has played these last ten years against South Africa, his last offered absolutely no chance for glamour or glory'.

It also presented Neil Adcock with a dilemma, since Denis was on a pair. 'Should I have tried like hell to get him out,' he recalls, 'or should he get one off the mark? I decided to try, but not too hard. Compo got an inside edge for one and we all felt better.' Not long afterwards Tayfield had him caught off bat and pad, for 5, by Russell Endean substituting for Johnny Waite behind the stumps. So ended the Test match career of a one-time prince reduced now to struggling against physical handicap.

Doug Insole on this tour was treasurer of the team's Saturday night club where it was assumed that anyone who had enjoyed a successful time at the races should chip in his mite. 'Here's a tenner,' Denis said one evening, claiming to have had just such a day during the fifth

Test. Then Frank Tyson appeared. 'Had a good day?' Insole enquired. 'Bloody awful,' came the reply, 'but not half as bad as Compo.'

Frank Tyson has supplied me with an interesting footnote to the tour of 1956/57. When his regular first-class career was finished, Denis went back to South Africa with a Commonwealth side to find himself more bogged down than ever by the persistent Tayfield. 'He made a supreme effort during one of the last games on the tour,' Frank says. 'In about an hour he lambasted Tayfield for about 70 runs, systematically hitting him past or over the head of every fielder from cover to deep square leg. Every time Tayfield moved a man it simply spurred Denis to negate the tactics. It was a quite brilliant display.'

1957: The Last Full Season

T HE CONSTRAINTS so long imposed upon him by that debilitating knee, not least the frustrations suffered on that tour of South Africa, led Denis to the conclusion that 1957 must be his last season although he subsequently agreed to be available to his county as an amateur. In a summer that also marked the end of the regular road for Bill Edrich, who was then to yield the county captaincy to John Warr, Jack Robertson, scoring more than 2,000 runs for the ninth time, enjoyed his best season since 1952. Jack followed this with a more than adequate performance in 1958 but then had such a wretched experience in 1959 that his retirement became both prudent and inevitable. A Middlesex era was certainly drawing to its close.

By his high standards Denis had an uneven, rather unpredictable summer which reflected the efforts of Middlesex overall. They finished seventh in the championship. Though he had to wait until mid-July before reaching three figures Denis lit the month of June with flashes of the old brilliance. Reg Simpson, recalling the last innings he saw him play, against Nottinghamshire, still enthuses about the way he stood back against Arthur Jepson, who was directing his attack on or outside the leg stump, to force him through and over the covers – 'and all on that groggy knee'. Denis followed with a scintillating 77 at Trent Bridge and then a score of 82 at Headingley, in his last match in Yorkshire.

In this innings, Denis would dearly have liked to score a further 18 runs. The match was one of the first that Don Wilson, the slow left-arm bowler, played for Yorkshire. Don, who went on to earn six Test appearances for England and is these days the head coach at Lord's, remembers how extremely nervous he was when brought on as third change to face his greatest hero. He was amazed, and suitably grateful, when Denis quietly pushed two full tosses down the pitch. 'Good luck, son,' Denis said to him at the end of the over. 'If you have as much fun out of this game as I have, you won't complain.'

At Kidderminster soon afterwards he made 48 and 82 against Worcestershire. In the first innings he struck the slow left hander, Bob Berry, for three sixes and five fours, needing only thirteen scoring shots altogether, and in the second only he was capable, according to *Wisden*, of forcing runs off the spin bowlers on a crumbling pitch.

His first hundred that summer was made against Lancashire at Old

Trafford, Denis galloping to the milestone with three sixes and eleven fours after Middlesex had lost their first three wickets for a pittance. He then ran himself out for 104. Next came his last Gentlemen v. Players match in which he was suitably honoured with the captaincy of the professionals.

The Players were reduced in their first innings to 46 for nine wickets, their lowest score for well over a hundred years, at which point the skipper deemed it wise to declare. Ted Dexter, who hitherto had taken only eighteen wickets in his first-class career, enjoyed the distinctively impressive figures of 5–2–8–5. He had Denis caught by Cowdrey at slip for 6, and he got him again in the second innings when the Players threatened to make the required 291 in three and three-quarter hours. In the end the pros, with nine wickets down, settled for a draw.

In his next county match, against Warwickshire at Edgbaston, Denis got 60 and 4 which in itself is nothing very remarkable. But it so happens that he twice fell victim to Jack Bannister who had previously bowled at him in 1955 at Lord's. On that occasion, the pitch wet and the ball flying, Denis came in, having just recovered from a broken finger, to give Bannister the charge. 'I dug it in, much nearer my end than his,' Jack reflects, 'and he gloved it to slip.' Compton c Dollery b Bannister 1.

In Compton's first innings against Bannister in 1957, Jack came back for a second spell and, letting go a 'half-volley loosener', was gratified to see it smashed straight down mid-wicket's throat. In the second innings he was yet more pleased to have Denis drag a ball on to his wicket from a mile outside the off stump. Jack now has the cherished memory of capturing Compton's wicket three times in eleven balls. No bad rabbit for the hutch.

In his next encounter, when Essex re-opened their old Leyton ground, Denis revealed no loss of the golden touch by making a brisk hundred in two and a quarter hours in Dickie Dodds' benefit match. An endearing touch of a different sort was evident in the following game at Hove, where Middlesex were all set to take the field against Sussex but found themselves short of their senior pro.

At 11.15 a.m. a telephone call from Bill Edrich revealed that Denis, who had stayed overnight with friends, apparently had overslept. Making a late appearance in gym shoes, he was put on to bowl as third change and finished off the opposition by taking five wickets, including those of Jim Parks, the Rev. David Sheppard and Hubert Doggart, for 40 runs. Even more satisfying for the Middlesex camp was Denis's performance on the second day. He arrived, more or less in good time, in the dressing room to announce that he had been advised of three 'certs' running that afternoon, 'and where can we find a bookmaker?' Unusually enough, all three horses won.

At Hove and in the three following fixtures he made no impact with the bat, but Middlesex had one more game to play, against Worcestershire at Lord's. In his last match as a professional cricketer for his county the maestro rose to the occasion.

He came out to bat on the first day when his side had lost two wickets for 76 on a bland pitch. Jack Robertson, then in his 41st year, was in elegant flow. The two of them shared a partnership of 225, with Denis making 143 before he was bowled by Jack Flavell. In an innings lasting just three hours, Denis hit one six and seventeen fours, the six a straight drive into the pavilion seats off Martin Horton which may have caught the attention of a four-year-old spectator, Patrick Compton. It was, as Ian Peebles attests, as if time had stood still – in all but one regard. Denis could no longer make his own length by adventuring down the pitch.

When he came out to bat in the second innings the applause began as soon as he emerged in the Long Room, and continued on a rising crescendo as he made his way to the middle with the old familiar, rolling gait. Everyone was on his feet, still cheering, when he took guard. It was an emotional, heart-warming reception evoking memories of the one that Patsy Hendren received when another great Middlesex cricketer played his last innings at Lord's in 1937. On this occasion Patsy was on official duty as the county's scorer.

In the second innings Denis, with 48 again, made top score for his side; a joyous celebration which ended with a juggling catch by 'Laddie' Outschoorn just inside the boundary boards at long-on. It was no bad way to go.

He finished his last full season with 1,404 runs in the championship, averaging 37.94 and yet again heading the Middlesex list, though only by a whisker from Jack Robertson who made 1,852 from seven matches more. Bill Edrich was third with 1, 016 at a modest 23.09.

Denis played in one further match in 1957, making 20 and 41 for the Rest of England against Surrey at Scarborough, when the county champions won by six wickets.

In the New Year's Honours list Denis Charles Scott Compton was made a CBE, an award greeted with universal delight. A wag in the Middlesex dressing room suggested that if ever he had difficulty in

159

remembering the details he had only to think of 'c and b Edrich'. By the turn of the year Denis also found himself richer by £2,000, the fruits of a testimonial marking his last full season with his beloved Middlesex.

1958 – 1964

Three more championship matches for Middlesex in 1958 bring the story of Denis's first-class career towards its end. At Lord's, in June, by which time he had passed his 40th birthday, he made 4 and 7 against Kent, batting in his old position at number 4. In early August he went in at number 6 behind Jack Robertson (4) and Bill Edrich (5) to score 31 against Hampshire at Portsmouth. He also took two wickets, one of them the satisfying scalp of Roy Marshall, then in his prime. Later in the month, he and Edrich played their last innings for the county at Lord's.

Even at that late stage of a miserable summer it was still by no means certain that Surrey would manage to win the championship for the seventh time in a row. Under a dashing new captain, Colin Ingleby-Mackenzie, Hampshire were enjoying the most successful season in their history. However, they could win only one of their last eight games and had to be content with second place, whereas Surrey came strongly to the finishing post. At Lord's on the third day against Middlesex, Surrey had the luck to find a pitch much to the liking of their celebrated spinners. Middlesex were bowled out in their second innings for 89, Jim Laker taking four wickets and Tony Lock five. Peter May then blazed Surrey to victory by six wickets with a very rapid innings of 47.

In the Middlesex first innings Bill Edrich made 15, and Denis two more. In the second, when Bill fell to Laker for nought, the challenge of old county adversaries and the problems posed by two great bowlers stimulated Denis's best competitive juices. He battled away for 21, *Wisden* recording that he had played splendidly. His was the one Middlesex wicket in that innings which did not go to either of the Surrey spin bowlers. He was caught behind off Alec Bedser – for the second time in the match. The Surrey wicket keeper was Arthur McIntyre who, twenty-six years earlier, had successfully represented London Elementary Schools on the same ground and found Denis's calling so lethal.

Denis's last appearance in 1958 was for Arthur Gilligan's XI against the New Zealanders at Hastings. He batted once for 24. A glance at *Wisden* reveals that he finished 12th in the Middlesex championship list and that Bill Edrich, who played eleven more games, did only marginally better. An asterisk against both their names denotes that they played as amateurs. In 1947 *Wisden* for the first time dropped the prefix of 'Mr' before the names of amateurs. The distinction between amateurs and professionals was finally abolished only in 1962.

When Denis went to Buckingham Palace to receive his CBE in 1958, it appears that the Queen asked him, 'How's your poor old head?' He was struggling for an answer, and wondering how Her Majesty could have heard about the party he had enjoyed the night before, when she explained that she was referring to the occasion when that ball from Ray Lindwall hit him on the head at Old Trafford in 1948.

Denis played in eight further first-class matches after 1958. In the following summer he got 71 at Fenner's for MCC against Cambridge University – a match in which a young undergraduate, Henry Blofeld, made an uninhibited 138. That was before Henry's most promising career was ended by a serious road accident.

In 1959 Denis captained a strong Commonwealth team, raised by Ron Roberts, in the Transvaal and his four innings included scores of 68 and 74 not out. In 1963 he played his last innings at Lord's: 87, with three sixes and eleven fours for MCC against Oxford University, not bad going for someone who must have forgotten when he had last taken a net and was by then playing only occasional light-hearted cricket.

In the following winter he captained another strong touring side, the Cavaliers, in Jamaica and took 103 (his 123rd and last hundred) off an attack which included Alfred Valentine and Frank Worrell. Finally, in 1964, at the age of 46, he went in at number 4 for MCC in a Lancashire centenary match at Old Trafford. Cyril Washbrook and Jack Ikin opened MCC's batting. In the second innings Denis enjoyed fruitful partnerships with Brian Close and Frank Worrell before being bowled by the leg-spinner Tommy Greenhough for 59.

Cricketing Stardom

WHEN DENIS was at the height of his fame and popularity his postbag was of such dimensions that even someone with the most orderly of minds would have been greatly taxed to cope with it. His locker in the Middlesex dressing room and the boot of his car were stuffed with letters, mostly asking for his autograph and/or photo but also including many requests to do this or that. Many of them, I think, were never even opened. A similar state of chaos prevailed on the circuit; Trevor Bailey says that Essex always knew they had followed Middlesex to a venue when they discovered further piles of mail addressed to the man of the hour. A national idol simply did not have the time to deal with it all unaided but, happily, some salvation, in the winter of 1948/49, was at hand.

On his first tour of South Africa, where his fan club was certainly no less zealous, he carried a suitcase full of letters into Reg Hayter's hotel bedroom and cried out for help. Reg, who was covering the tour for Reuter's, assumed at first that the basic requirement was to sort out a method whereby requests for Denis's signature might be met. On going through the pile, however, he discovered a letter from the editor of the *News of the World*, postmarked several months earlier, which proposed that Denis should write a weekly column for them. Not only that; Reg also unearthed another, much more recent, letter from the same editor which said, more or less, and not unreasonably, that since Mr Compton had not answered the first letter, the offer was withdrawn.

At a further meeting, Reg was asked by Denis if he would take on the management of his business affairs. But Reg at that time was a full-time cricket reporter needing to remain independent; it was still some years before he set up his own highly successful sporting press agency off Fleet Street and from that diversified into player management. However, when Reg returned home from South Africa he happened to meet Bagenal Harvey, who was then the director of a company in the film business, and told him the story of a famous cricketer desperately in need of guidance. 'The time has more than come,' Bagenal suggested with some perception, 'for sportsmen to be properly represented.'

In due course Reg and Bagenal had a meeting with Denis at Reg's home in Brondesbury, and a deal was struck. Reg and Denis then went off to watch some boxing. 'What about this chap Bagenal?' Denis asked.

'Do you trust him?' 'There's no problem so far as I know,' Reg replied. 'Anyway, you've agreed already.' Nor was there a problem. Denis became front runner in what was to become a sporting empire, initially over a trial period but soon on a permanent basis. As his agency commission, Bagenal took 10 per cent, a rate that was never increased.

One of the first tasks of the newly formed Bagenal Harvey Organisation was to sort out and catch up with Denis's mail, a job which occupied Bagenal's secretary for several weeks. Another was to find compensation for the loss of regular income from the *News of the World*. Bagenal approached Hugh Cudlipp, editor of the *Sunday Express*, who was happy to do a deal. Denis, with a typical sense of loyalty, insisted that Reg Hayter, rather than a staff man, should be his ghost writer, and the editor, still in agreement, asked Reg what he would want for the job. Reg was then earning about £16 a week. 'I thought I had nothing to lose,' he tells me. 'I said £20 for each piece. They paid up.'

Reg recalls that the first column included one rather esoteric word of four syllables (he can't now remember which one) which caused some pleasure in the Middlesex dressing room on Monday morning. Jack Young, always an expert in abstruse language, asked the supposed author what exactly the word meant. ' — if I know,' Denis replied. 'Why?'

It is worth noting that Reg Hayter produced a very readable Sunday column under Denis's name for the best part of a decade without ever needing to show it first to Middlesex or MCC. A responsible professional journalist had the common sense to know how far he could go without getting Denis into official trouble or upsetting other players. There were never any problems. Forty years on, Denis is still contributing his weekly Sunday piece. It has been a happy association, now by some way the longest between a national newspaper and a big sporting name. The *Sunday Express* marked his 70th birthday last year by sending him over to Augusta to enjoy the Masters, a generous gesture made even more appealing by Sandy Lyle's victory in the tournament.

I want now to put the clock back to 1948, before Bagenal Harvey appeared on the sporting scene. In that year Denis was invited by Bill Crossley, creative director of the Royds advertising agency, to play a starring role in the Brylcreem advertising campaign which had already projected the handsome features of Richard Greene – television's Robin Hood – on the nation's billboards. The unique feature of this campaign was that the identity of the individual was never explicitly stated; a trick that worked well for many years all over the world. It was characteristic of Denis that after receiving an offer of £1,000 a year from George Royds, in the latter's Piccadilly office, he should have gone straight to Gubby Allen to find out how Middlesex would react. Gubby, and the county committee, could see no objection, but there can be no doubt that even mild reservations on their part would have persuaded Denis to turn the offer down.

It says much for Denis's charisma that in the course of a long-running and very successful campaign his name is the one, more than any other, which those of us with longer memories still associate with Brylcreem. We are able to recall that fine head of hair, smoothed by the magic unguent, and contrast it with its more dishevelled state on most occasions. Yet the Brylcreem celebrity list was an extensive one: the actors Robert Beatty and Roger Moore, broadcaster, author and journalist John Arlott and, from the world of cricket, Godfrey Evans, Keith Miller, Ray Lindwall, Fazal Mahmood and Arthur Milton. Arthur also represented football, as did Nat Lofthouse and Johnny Haynes. Dai Rees and Gary Player carried the flag for golf.

Denis still had four more seasons of first-class cricket left when, in 1953, he branched out into a new part-time activity which was to provide him with an important, stable base in the years ahead. The initiative came from George Royds' son, Nicholas, who was very much involved in running the Beecham account, including Brylcreem, at the agency. Denis joined forced with Royds as a public relations executive looking after Beecham's sporting interests and soon proved himself to be a most effective catalyst. He played a key role in the creation of the County Cup, later known as the Brylcreem Cup, which was awarded monthly for the best performance in a county game. Jimmy Hill, then secretary of the footballers' Players' Union, went round the country in the summer presenting the trophy to the winners.

Royds, as may be gathered from the names of those who were associated with Brylcreem, quickly built itself a reputation as *the* sportsman's advertising agency; it was no coincidence that all its directors were keen sportsmen themselves, and it never had much difficulty in turning out an unbeatable cricket side.

In assessing Denis's commercial attributes, Nicholas Royds says that he always had a very good understanding of the market and of what made people tick. 'He understands *people*. He's an absolute democrat with no side, no humbug and no politics.' (This of course has nothing to do with his views on politicians meddling in sport, a subject to which I shall shortly turn.) It is certain that Nicholas and Denis made a very successful partnership both on and off the golf course. In 1963 Denis became a director of Royds Public Relations company and, with his understanding of clients' requirements, made an excellent fist of it. In the mid-70s, when Royds set up a subsidiary company, Durden-Smith Communications, Denis joined Neil Durden-Smith on its board. Towards the end of that decade, Royds sold out their entire business to Extel, Denis staying with it for seven more years before Extel sold Royds to McCann-Erickson in 1986. With McCann-Erickson Denis loyally remains.

In the days when Denis worked for Royds in Mandeville Place, not far north of Oxford Street, he would collect a pile of parking tickets in his office as evidence of the fact the he had left his car, open and unlocked, on yellow lines outside the front entrance. On other occasions, he blocked the back entrance of Findlaters, the wine merchants, then also a subsidiary of Beecham.

For many years Nicholas's secretary, Shirley Smith, liaised with Christine, Bagenal Harvey's secretary (who was to become Denis's third wife), in a joint effort to keep Denis's diary of engagements on an orderly footing. He has never, so far as I know, kept a diary himself – and a few of the dates willingly agreed to as he moved around might with luck be subsequently recorded in one office or the other. This explains how those who know him well have long been prudent enough to get an appointment written in and endorsed at secretarial level. But even this, though no fault of Shirley or Christine, could never be regarded as a fail-safe system, and matters could be quite chaotic when those expecting him to turn up for something or other had neglected to check in at base.

There was a time, Shirley Smith remembers, when Denis got himself billed to appear in two charity cricket matches, a long way apart, on the same day. He eventually turned up for a pro-am golf tournament to which he had not been officially invited.

I can understand how the organisers felt, having had a similar experience myself. It was disturbing to find out that after agreeing to play for an MCC side against my old school, Cranbrook, Denis, with his endearing inability to say 'no' to anybody, had pledged himself to appear in two other games at the same time. I felt obliged to take a very firm line about this major difficulty. It stands greatly to his credit that having driven from Buckinghamshire to Kent through the heart of London, he arrived only five minutes late.

I must record one more memory of Denis's days at Mandeville Place.

Shirley Smith says that he *never* put in for any expenses, travel, subsistence and the like, incurred in the line of duty. She had to go through the diary to discover what he should rightly claim. Nicholas further adds that Denis even then was embarrassed to accept reimbursement!

It might be added that the problems posed by Denis's sackful of mail were never wholly solved. Peter Parfitt asserts that when he returned to Middlesex in 1959, after completing his service in the RAF, he took over Denis's locker in the dressing room to find amongst its chaotic disarray a number of cheques dating back to the Compton benefit ten years earlier.

In 1959 Denis added another string to his bow when he joined BBC television's cricket commentary team. For more than a decade he retained a large and loyal following. He was then 'dropped' without even, I believe, an official explanation or a letter of thanks from the hierarchy for his services. Another old colleague of mine, Brian Johnston, suffered a similar fate at the same time. It was a woeful example of declining standards, and neither of them has forgiven BBC television for the manner of their going. Brian, at least, could return to his natural métier, radio, but Denis, without such an obvious outlet, had to content himself with his regular columns for the *Sunday Express*.

The reasons for the BBC's decision could be understood even though they won no prizes for the way in which it was implemented. It was thought that as an interpolator Denis did not consistently provide the thoughtful analysis required.

He was of course one of those marvellously gifted players who never had to think profoundly about the game. Without need for a net, he could rise from his slumbers in the dressing room, borrow someone else's bat and go out to make a hundred. From the commentary box he knew exactly what batsmen and bowlers were thinking but his thoughts on general tactics, on what should be going through a captain's mind, were less penetrating. He was never quite cast for the cool and clinical approach, and he was sometimes inspired by the milk of human kindness to make judgements more tolerant and less forthright than he would offer these days.

As a colleague throughout his television days, I always found him utterly loyal and enormous fun to work with, but, needless to say, it could not be guaranteed that he would be unfailingly punctual. I remember an occasion during a Test match at Trent Bridge when we resumed our broadcast after lunch. There was no sign of Denis, who may well have had a pressing engagement with his bookmaker, so our producer, Philip Lewis, devised a scenario to get his own back.

When Denis at last turned up, a stage manager announced that the editor of *Grandstand* in London required him to give an immediate three-minute summary of the morning's play. In steady rain a chastened Denis mounted a perpendicular ladder to the in-vision position, sat down in front of a camera and was at once cued to do his thing. Sadly, there appeared to be no umbrella available. Denis had got about two-thirds of the way through his ordeal when a pair of headphones was thrust around his ears. 'I'd just like you to know, Compo,' Philip Lewis said from the comfort of his production scanner, 'that you haven't been "live" and we just thought we'd record it for our own amusement. But you did very well in testing circumstances.'

Life After Cricket

WHEN DENIS's second marriage, to Valerie, came to an end in 1960, she returned to her native country, South Africa, with legal arrangements made for their elder son, Richard, to be in his mother's charge and for Patrick to be in his father's. So Richard also returned to Durban, but Patrick remained in England until he had left Marlborough College. He subsequently went to Rhodes University and stayed on to make a career in the Republic.

For most of Patrick's days through prep and public school his father had the problem of keeping a young man happy in his holidays and providing him with a stable base. So Denis was very grateful at that time to have formed a close friendship with Tommy and Viv Wallis. He first met them at one of Stan Joel's charity cricket matches and if I add that Tommy is managing director of the Racecourse Holdings Trust, it is easy to perceive an interest they all had in common from the outset.

The Wallis's house in Camberley became a second home for Patrick, and the two Wallis sons, John and Stephen, practised morning, noon and night with Patrick in a cricket net on the back lawn. John Wallis and Patrick were regular attenders at the Lord's Easter coaching classes. In the summer they would turn up outside the Grace Gates to collect tickets supposedly left for them by Denis, and were rarely surprised to find themselves waiting until he arrived at the eleventh hour. Patrick was a very promising cricketer but one, of course, with the hardest possible act to follow. In due course he spent four summers in the Marlborough XI, heading their batting averages three times and their bowling twice. He may even have had greater potential as a tennis player.

'He was an intellectual,' Viv Wallis reports, 'and a lot of things his father would have liked to be. He inherited some of his father's faults including unpunctuality and an ability to lose almost anything.' He is also, like an echo of his dashing father, a handsome young man with a relaxed and natural charm. I believe that his brother Richard is thought by the ladies to be even better looking. John Warr's wife, Valerie, says she goes quite wobbly at the knees in his company.

*   *   *

No one was more distressed than Denis when MCC cancelled their tour of South Africa in 1968/69 after the Republic's government had refused to accept Basil D'Oliviera as a member of the English party. Denis fell in love with South Africa – though certainly not with the subsequent declaration of apartheid – when he first toured in 1948/49. He has remained staunchly loyal to his many friends there, believing that their national Cricket Union has done all that has been asked of it by the International Cricket Conference to ensure that the game is genuinely multi-racial. He has consistently and vigorously made his views known in print and on the air. So it came as no surprise that he should be closely identified with the attempt in 1983 to get MCC to send their own touring side to South Africa the following winter.

The initiative for such a venture was taken by the Freedom in Sport organization led by the Conservative MP John Carlisle, one of five men on its executive committee who were also members of MCC. They were not at all exercised to find another forty-five like-minded members, including Denis and Bill Edrich, to produce the necessary number for demanding a special general meeting. In due course Denis and Bill, along with John Carlisle, were pictured at Lord's presenting a petition to Jack Bailey, the MCC Secretary. It proposed that MCC's committee should implement the selection of a touring party in 1983/84. John Carlisle later conceded that it may have been a mistake to put a date to the venture; it was more important at that stage to establish a principle.

MCC's committee were put on the spot. To select first-class players would have brought about immediate sanctions. To send out any sort of official team would have been in breach of the Gleneagles Agreement. Moreover, although MCC no longer lent their name to England teams overseas, and had not done so since 1976/77, the three famous letters remained synonymous with England in the cricket world at large.

A special general meeting of MCC was held in the Westminster Hall on the evening of 13 July 1983, not long after India had beaten West Indies in the final of the third World Cup. About 1,000 members attended on an intensely hot evening; at least twice as many had been expected. The motion was cogently proposed by John Carlisle. Hubert Doggart and Colin Cowdrey spoke persuasively against it on behalf of MCC's committee. Denis and Brian Johnston were amongst those who supported the proposal from the floor and David Sheppard, Bishop of Liverpool, was in the ranks of those who spoke against it.

The motion was lost in the hall by 535 votes to 439, and through the post by 6,604 to 4,344. If the result disappointed Denis and his allies, there was no denying that 40 per cent of those who voted, comprising not far short of a quarter of MCC's membership, had opposed their committee on this issue. So far as Denis is concerned, the fight to restore cricketing links with South Africa continues unabated.

*　　　*　　　*

Misguided though we may be, those of us getting on in years may feel entitled in our intolerance to believe that things are not what they used to be, and may even in some respects have gone to the dogs. Denis has little time for what the so-called 'Packer revolution' did for cricket, nor indeed for the crucial part played in it by Tony Greig, who was England's captain at the time. He concedes that it transformed the income of top players but believes that it has encouraged some of them to get their priorities confused. He likes limited-overs cricket, in moderation, but considers that it has much to answer for in its influence on the traditional game; it has encouraged negative bowling and too much unsound batting technique. This is not to say that with his own unique gifts for improvisation he would not have relished the challenges of the abbreviated game.

He cannot understand, having always used a lightweight bat himself (2 lb 2 oz), how the modern batsman prefers a heavy bludgeon – and this is supported, I am sure, by almost all of his contemporaries. Never a stranger to bouncers in his own prime, he is dismayed by the consistent intimidation that may be observed today, by the failure of umpires to enforce the law and by the failure of administrators to support the umpires when they do.

He is not impressed by the way many batsmen, in seeking to evade the bouncer, take their eyes off the ball, and he insists that if he played today he would never contemplate wearing a helmet or any other protection beyond the traditional items. He never even wore a thigh pad.

He gets bored, as so many of us do, with an unchanging diet of seam bowling, deplores present-day over rates – now a little better in Test matches but still not good enough – and remembers with a feeling of nostalgic regret the time when it was the norm for a side to field a balanced attack.

I must be careful not to give an impression that Denis, the most positive of cricketers himself, takes a wholly negative view of the modern game. He can be as thrilled as anybody by an innings from Viv Richards or an exemplary piece of bowling by Richard Hadlee. But above all he believes that today's cricketers don't get half the fun out of the game that he did, and in that I suspect he is absolutely right.

*   *   *

In February 1987, shortly after Mike Gatting's side had retained the Ashes in Australia, Denis was the subject of Thames Television's *This is Your Life*. They had wanted to feature him on the programme many years earlier but found, as I understand, that his second wife Valerie declined to cooperate. Now, by relating more or less in order of appearance how the programme unrolled, I can catch up with some family details.

All three of his sons, Brian (by his first marriage, to Doris), Richard and Patrick were flown over from South Africa. Brian is a personnel director in Johannesburg and Richard and Patrick are journalists in Durban. Christine, who married Denis in 1975, was next to appear, followed by their elder daughter Charlotte, who her mother said had arrived in this world at about the time when stumps were drawn in the Centenary Test at Lord's in 1980. Since Charlotte at the time of the programme was nine years old, there must have been a slight family confusion about dates, but no matter. The next picture on our screens was a touching film of Victoria, aged two, waving happily to a father whose reciprocal, natural greeting she could not possibly have seen.

Later in the programme, Hilda, Denis's sister, recalled what encouragement her two brothers had received from a father who had been so keen to see them prosper in their chosen professions, and we met Diane, widow of Leslie, who had died in 1984. Later still, at the climax of the show, Denis's eldest grandchildren, Craig, 20, and Elizabeth, made their bow. Little Victoria then made a stunning solo entrance and, finally, Richard rushed offstage to return with his wife Glynis, their son Nicholas (4) and their two-month-old baby daughter Alexandra, asleep in her mother's arms and now seen by her grandfather for the first time. All this brought things to an emotional conclusion which I think brought the hint of a tear or two in Denis's eyes.

John Warr was moved to enquire later whether Craig, Denis's eldest grandson at 20, would now be calling Victoria 'auntie'. Godfrey Evans, the first distinguished sportsman to make an entry, took one look at the substantial Compton family assembled and suggested how wise he had been, when facing Lindwall and Miller without a box in 1948, to hasten off the field for essential equipment.

Some old black and white film footage revealed Denis reaching his hundredth 100 – and the rapid, confident, perfectly poised footwork with which he loved to play slow bowling. There was also footage from his two famous Test hundreds in 1948 which ended with a shot of him disturbing the stumps at Trent Bridge as he fell headlong in evading a bouncer from Miller: the perfect cue to introduce his old adversary who had flown from Australia. The reunion of two great friends was another touching moment. Was the bouncer, Eamonn asked, a signal from Keith to Denis that one of Scobie Breasley's tips had turned up trumps?

Next, there came a tribute from Sir Leonard Hutton who greatly regretted that he could not be present but sent a message recorded at his home on film. Recalling that they had played their first Test match together fifty years earlier, he said, 'I so admired your approach, your sense of humour and the way you played. You were the most popular player of my generation.' Four other old Test colleagues, Peter May, Alec Bedser, Trevor Bailey and Fred Trueman, then made their entrance. I suspect it was the only programme, radio or television, that Fred has appeared in without uttering a single word.

England's latest captain sent his filmed tribute from Australia. 'Your name, Denis, was always an inspirational one in the Gatting household. My brother Steve went to Arsenal, I went to Middlesex, and *you* did both.'

Denis's footballing days were evoked with film of him scoring a humdinger of a goal for Arsenal against Bolton in the quarter-final round of the FA Cup in 1950, and of his pass which enabled Ted Lewis to score in their victory over Liverpool in the Cup Final at Wembley. This was the cue for Joe Mercer, his captain that day, to appear but many will have felt disappointed that he was not asked for an anecdote.

Then it was back to cricket again, and Gubby Allen remembering on film how Denis had disobeyed his instructions when playing his first innings for Middlesex, and then getting a 'terrible decision'. That gave Denis his chance to say that the umpire had been dying for a pee. Ted Dexter remembered asking for his first autograph when he went to

Lord's as a prep school boy in 1947. 'Denis said "no" – but he did it with his unfailing charm.'

The roll of England cricketers invited to honour Denis was completed by John Warr, Don Wilson, Alan Oakman, Fred Rumsey, Colin Milburn and Doug Insole. Another old friend, the former Hampshire captain, Colin Ingleby-Mackenzie, could share his love of the gee-gees with the man of the moment. The same might be said of four very special friends – Ted Woodward (an England Rugby international), Dr Jim Murphy-O'Connor (likewise with Ireland), Louis Stalder (Wasps' Rugby) and John Sheridan (professional at Denham Golf Club) – known as the Four Musketeers.

Ted Woodward reported that they were all at Denis's home one afternoon when their host suggested putting thirty quid from the housekeeping money on a strongly tipped horse, Wayward Lad, at 10 to 1. The others had already backed it. 'Use the telephone in the kitchen, but for God's sake do it quietly,' he urged. The horse was pipped at the post after looking a winner for most of the course. 'I think,' Ted reflected, 'that Denis's reaction summed up his attitude to life. "Ah well," he said, "let's have another bottle of bubbly." '

I have left until last one unexpected tribute paid to Denis on the programme; it came on film from Islamabad, from none other than President Zia of Pakistan. 'I was an officer cadet in India in 1944,' he told Denis, 'and you were a good teacher and a good friend. I found you a noble person who believed in the dignity of man and in your love and affection for human beings.' Denis must, I think, have been the first subject of a *This is Your Life* programme to be acclaimed by a head of state.

At the end of it all, when the programme credits had rolled, Denis said, 'This is the most moving and probably the most memorable night I'll ever know. I've got my *whole* family together for the first time, and all my friends. And I never knew anything about it.'

*   *   *

On 23 May 1988 the Beecham Group and Middlesex County Cricket Club celebrated Denis's 70th birthday with a dinner attended by some 750 people at the Intercontinental Hotel in London. It was an emotional occasion enjoyed not just by his old contemporaries in the game but by a host of supporters who simply wanted to pay tribute to an old hero. Thames Television took the opportunity to mount a special programme introduced by Ian Wooldridge.

Benny Green, Colin Cowdrey, Peter Parfitt and J. J. Warr all made felicitous speeches, and Denis, rounding things off in characteristically modest fashion, included a favoured story about Fred Trueman who once had Lindsay Hassett caught by the Rev David Sheppard. "Ard luck, Lindsay,' said Fred. 'Once a Rev puts his hands together, you've got no bluddy chance.'

Benny Green told us that the main influences in his life had been Duke Ellington, Frank Sinatra and Denis Compton – though not necessarily in that order. The Middlesex and England left-hander, Peter Parfitt, elaborated a theme well known to those who know of his after-dinner gifts by recalling the day at Lord's when he was first chosen as Middlesex's twelfth man.

'The hour for play is approaching,' he said, 'and there is *no* sign of a certain contracted player. At 11.25 precisely the two umpires are on their way out to the middle. At about 11.28 the fielding side have joined them, and our two opening batsmen prepare to take the field. At 11.30 precisely the door of our dressing room opens and Mr Compton enters – in 'iis dinner jacket. "Twelfers," he enquires, "what are we doing?" "We're batting," I say, whereupon he goes to a corner of the room and sits down on his settee. In due course he changes into his cricket gear, applies a touch of Brylcreem to his head and sits down again. "Twelfers," he says. "Wake me up when it's time for me to go in." '

I am content in writing about a living legend to let Peter Parfitt have the penultimate word. The last I leave to Ian Wooldridge who explained in one of his scintillating columns in the *Daily Mail* how his newspaper planned to give Denis, for his 70th birthday present, the old Warsop bat he had used in 1947.

Ian discovered that according to Denis the bat had been handed over at the end of that season to the boss of the Warsop family, but a search through their archives proved fruitless. Ian was still seeking to run it to earth when a nice lady on the MCC switchboard suggested he try the Lord's Memorial Gallery. 'No problem,' came back the answer. 'Denis Compton presented it to us in 1956, and it's been on display here ever since.'

Statistics

COMPILED BY DEREK LODGE

Denis Compton in Test Cricket

Season	Opponents	Innings	N.O.	H.S.	Runs	Average	100	50
1937	N. Zealand	1	0	65	65	65.00	–	1
1938	Australia	6	1	102	214	42.80	1	1
1939	W. Indies	5	2	120	189	63.00	1	–
1946	India	4	2	71*	146	73.00	–	2
1946/47	Australia	10	1	147	459	51.00	2	2
1946/47	N. Zealand	1	0	38	38	38.00	–	–
1947	S. Africa	8	0	208	753	94.12	4	2
1948	Australia	10	1	184	562	62.44	2	2
1948/49	S. Africa	9	1	114	406	50.75	1	2
1949	N. Zealand	6	0	116	300	50.00	2	–
1950	W. Indies	2	0	44	55	27.50	–	–
1950/51	Australia	8	1	23	53	7.57	–	–
1950/51	N. Zealand	3	0	79	107	35.66	–	1
1951	S. Africa	6	0	112	312	52.00	1	2
1952	India	4	2	35*	59	29.50	–	–
1953	Australia	8	1	61	234	33.42	–	2
1953/54	W. Indies	7	0	133	348	49.71	1	2
1954	Pakistan	5	0	278	453	90.60	1	2
1954/55	Australia	7	2	84	191	38.20	–	1
1955	S. Africa	9	0	158	492	54.66	1	3
1956	Australia	2	1	94	129	129.00	–	1
1956/57	S. Africa	10	0	64	242	24.20	–	2

	Opponents	Innings	N.O.	H.S.	Runs	Average	100	50
	Australia	51	8	184	1842	42.83	5	9
	S. Africa	42	1	208	2205	53.78	7	11
	W. Indies	14	2	133	592	49.33	2	2
	N. Zealand	11	0	116	510	46.36	2	2
	India	8	4	71*	205	51.25	–	2
	Pakistan	5	0	278	453	90.60	1	2
	In England	76	10	278	3963	60.04	13	18
	Abroad	55	5	147	1844	36.88	4	10
	Total	**131**	**15**	**278**	**5807**	**50.06**	**17**	**28**

Bowling: Balls 2716   Runs 1410   Wickets 25   Average 56.40
Catches: 49

Achievements:

1938   Youngest man to score a century for England: 102 v. Australia, aged 20 years 19 days.

1946/47   Scored 147 and 103* v. Australia at Adelaide, the fifth man to score two hundreds in a Test for England, after C.A.G. Russell, H. Sutcliffe (twice), W. R. Hammond and E. Paynter. Nobody has done so since, for England, in 42 years.

1947   Compton's 753 in the series remains the record aggregate for an Englishman playing in England. He scored four centuries; among Englishmen, only H. Sutcliffe (twice) and W. R. Hammond have equalled this.

1948   His aggregate of 562 was, at the time, the record for an Englishman playing against Australia, in England. It has since been beaten by D. I. Gower, in 1985.

1954   His 278 is the record score in a Test at Trent Bridge. He reached his 200 in 245 minutes, the second fastest by an Englishman. W. R. Hammond, playing against New Zealand at Auckland in 1932/33, reached 200 just five minutes quicker.

Compton's 2205 against South Africa is the record for a player of any nationality against that country.

Denis Compton in first-class cricket

Season	Innings	N.O.	H.S.	Runs	Average	100	50
1936	32	3	100*	1004	34.62	1	8
1937	46	4	177	1980	47.14	3	16
1938	47	6	180*	1868	45.56	5	8
1939	50	6	214*	2468	56.09	8	11
1944/45 (in India)	13	2	249*	990	90.00	5	2
1945/46 (in India)	4	0	124	316	79.00	2	1
1946	45	6	235	2403	61.61	10	10
1946/47 (M.C.C. in Australia)	25	3	163	1432	65.09	5	8
1946/47 (M.C.C. in N. Zealand)	6	1	97*	228	45.60	–	1
1947	50	8	246	3816	90.85	18	12
1948	47	7	252*	2451	61.27	9	8
1948/49 (M.C.C. in S. Africa)	26	5	300	1781	84.80	8	4
1949	56	4	182	2530	48.65	9	11
1950	23	2	144	957	45.57	2	4
1950/51 (M.C.C. in Australia)	21	5	142	882	55.12	4	2
1950/51 (M.C.C. in N. Zealand)	5	0	79	213	42.60	–	2

1951	40	6	172	2193	64.50	8	9
1952	54	6	132	1880	39.16	4	10
1953	47	5	143*	1659	39.50	4	12
1953/54 (M.C.C. in W. Indies)	14	1	133	630	48.46	1	4
1954	28	2	278	1524	58.61	4	9
1954/55 (M.C.C. in Australia)	16	2	182	799	57.07	3	3
1955	36	1	158	1209	34.54	2	6
1956	21	1	110	705	35.25	2	3
1956/57 (M.C.C. in S. Africa)	22	1	131	792	37.71	2	5
1957	45	0	143	1554	34.53	3	9
1958	6	0	31	104	17.33	–	–
1959	2	0	71	107	53.50	–	1
1959/60 (S. Africa)	4	1	74*	160	53.33	–	2
1963	2	0	87	88	44.00	–	1
1963/64 (W. Indies)	4	0	103	146	36.50	1	–
1964	2	0	59	73	36.50	–	1
Total	**839**	**88**	**300**	**38942**	**51.85**	**123**	**183**

County Championship, for Middlesex

	455	45	252*	20174	49.20	62	101

Bowling: (first-class) 622 wickets, average 32.27
Catches: 415

Achievements:

1936   1000 in the season of his debut. Some thirty players have done this, but Compton remains the youngest to do so.

1937   He scored 1980 runs in the season. If he had made 20 more, he would have been easily the youngest player to score 2000 in a season. Hutton, two years older than Compton, became the holder of that record, also in 1937, but was overtaken by G. A. Hick in 1986; he was 287 days younger than Hutton, at the dates of their completing 2000 runs. Compton did score 2000 in 1939, and remains the third-youngest to do so.

1946/47   He scored four consecutive hundreds in Australia. The record is six consecutive centuries, but comparatively few players have managed four, and only A. R. Border, W. R. Hammond, C. G. Macartney and P. B. H. May have, like Compton, achieved it on tour. E. de C. Weekes scored five consecutive hundreds when on tour in New Zealand.

1947   He scored 3816 runs and 18 hundreds in the season, both records which may well stand for ever. He made 1187 runs against the South Africans, another record, and scored 2048 runs at Lord's, the record aggregate by one player on any ground in a season. In the calendar year of 1947, he scored 4962 runs, yet another record.

1948 He and W. J. Edrich added 424 in four hours against Somerset at Lord's, the fifth highest third-wicket stand in first-class cricket, and the highest unbroken stand. His captain, F. G. Mann, declared with fifty minutes of the first day remaining, and Middlesex almost won in two days.

1948/49 His 300 against North-Eastern Transvaal at Benoni, in 181 minutes, was the fastest triple-century in first-class cricket. Compton scored 180 before lunch on the second day. His aggregate of 1781 remained the record for a season in South Africa until J. R. Reid of New Zealand scored 1915 in 1961/62.

Between the start of the 1946 season, and his knee injury in 1950, Compton scored 15034 runs, at an average of 66.22, with 60 centuries.

Index